A List of Emigrant Ministers to America,
1690—1811

A LIST OF
EMIGRANT MINISTERS
TO AMERICA

1690—1811

BY
GERALD FOTHERGILL

JANAWAY PUBLISHING, INC.
Santa Maria, California

Notice

In many older books, foxing (or discoloration) occurs and, in some instances, print lightens with wear and age. Reprinted books, such as this, often duplicate these flaws, notwithstanding efforts to reduce or eliminate them. The pages of this reprint have been digitally enhanced and, where possible, the flaws eliminated in order to provide clarity of content and a pleasant reading experience.

A List of Emigrant Ministers to America 1690-1811

Originally published:
London, 1904

Reprinted by

Janaway Publishing, Inc.
732 Kelsey Ct.
Santa Maria, California 93454
(805) 925-1038
www.janawaygenealogy.com

2015

ISBN: 978-1-59641-360-3

Made in the United States of America

INTRODUCTION

To List of Ministers and Schoolmasters of the Church of England who went to the Western Colonies, having received a Bounty of Twenty Pounds from the King in order to Defray Cost of the Passage

THE object of this work has been to present in handy form for the historian, genealogist, and biographer a list of those who received the bounty.

The Treasury books for this date not being calendared, the exact origin of how this passage money came to be paid has not been discovered, nor has the actual warrant from the King to the Treasury, mentioned in the following letter from the Bishop of London to the Treasury, been found:

'*June* 23, 1721. *John, Bishop of London, to the Lords of the Treasury.*

' The Bishop of London was by King Charles II. entrusted with providing and sending ministers to the colonies and islands in America, and was directed by King William to apply to the Treasury for £20 to each missionary to defray his passage. This bounty was readily paid. Afterwards it was ofttimes delayed, and many of the missionaries were reduced to great straits. At present the answer given them is that several to whom the bounty has been given did not proceed on the mission, and therefore their Lordships made a difficulty to grant the same any longer.

' Hopes there was little ground for the remark in his predecessor's time. Although he once lost £20 of his own money, he has not lost any of His Majesty's, except in one instance, where the party fell into madness and was not suffered to go. Two persons who lately had the £20 did not proceed, but after their despatch at the Treasury they got preferment at home, and one of them refunded the £20, which he (the Bishop) applied to another missionary without troubling their Lordships; the other has paid back one-half, and the remainder is daily expected, and he would apply it in the same way. But if (as there seems some reason to apprehend) their Lordships think it not fit to trust him any longer with this dispensation, presumes they will move His Majesty to employ some other person, for if this bounty were retrenched it would be impossible to get those colonies supplied. In that case, shall willingly acquiesce in the conviction that he has faithfully and honestly done his duty. This comfortable reflection has hitherto relieved him against malicious slanders, and will continue to do so, especially as he shall be freed from a great and vexatious trouble, which has no connection with the duty of a Bishop of London.'—'Treasury Papers,' vol. 234, folio 36.

An earlier mention that King William granted this bounty is to be found in this extract from the 'Treasury Papers':

'King William III. gave twenty pounds to each minister and schoolmaster going to the Western Colonies, and this was continued by her late Majesty—October 29, 1714.'— Vol. 181, folio 32.

The procedure adopted to obtain the grant was as follows: The Bishop of London would, by letter, ask for the bounty, and the Lords of the Treasury would then issue a warrant to the Receipt of the Exchequer for the payment; one form of the Bishop's letter is appended and two examples of warrant:

'*May* 26, 1690.'

'My Lords,
    'Mr. Gelibrand going over Chaplain for New York withe Collonel Sclater I would humbly intreat yor Lord^{ps} to let Collonel Sclater have ye King's benevolence of twenty pounds for his voyage.
    'My Lords,
        'Yo^r Lord^p most obedient sert.,
            'H. London.'

'By virtue of the General Letters Patent Dormant bearing date the 8th April, 1689. These are to pray and require you to draw one or more orders for payment unto Ar. Low, Clerk, of the sum of £20 without account in reward of his service and satisfaction for the charges of his Transportation to the Leward Islands whither he is going Chaplain 3 May, 1695.'—Money Book, 12-504.

'After a^c By virtue of H.M. General Letters Patent Dormant bearing date the 22nd of June, 1727. These are to pray and require your Lordship to draw an order for paying unto

Emigrant Ministers to America

Jeremiah Leaming the sum of £20 without account towards defraying the charge of his passage to the Province of New England in America, whither he is going a Minister according to the Certificate of the Lord Bishop of London hereunto annexed, and let the same be satisfied out of any money in the Receipt of the Exchequer applicable to the use of his Majesty's Civil Government, for which this shall be your Lordship's Warrant. Whitehall Treasury Chambers the 13th day of July, 1748.'

The materials for this list have been obtained from classes of records known as Money Books, King's Warrant Books, Treasury Papers, and Exchequer of Receipt Papers, all now preserved in the Public Record Office.

The value of the fact that a warrant was issued for the payment of the £20 is that it shows the Bishop of London had appointed the payee to some definite cure in the colonies, and no doubt in the majority of cases the recipient went to his preferment; the reports of the Society for the Propagation of the Gospel show that many who received the benevolence had been born in the colonies, and had been to England for Holy Orders, so that each individual name in this book must depend on outside evidence to determine the natal place of the emigrant; if after some research in American or colonial records a clergyman totally disappears, and his name is in these pages at an earlier date than the one on which he was last known on the other side, it seems in that case presumptive evidence that he was a native of England and left these shores for the first time. In this way these contents may save much useless searching in America and the colonies when the research ought to be on this side. Another use that can be made is to trace removals of clergymen, which is very often a difficult genealogical feat. Appended are instances:

'Francis Hoyland went to S. Christopher in 1754, and in 1769 a Francis Hoyland went to S. Carolina.'

'Brian Hunt, 1709-10, to Barbadoes, and in 1722 to Virginia.'

This book will be found of further value in correction and annotation of biographical works. For instance:

'Sprague says that Tho. Craddock came to America in 1742'; but he did not receive the bounty till 1743-1744.

Also, additions can be made, for Sprague mentions:

'That it is not improbable that Hugh Jones paid a visit to

England in 1722, for he had left Virginia, and in 1728 he published a book in London.'

This was so, as this list shows that he returned to Virginia September 18, 1724; and in the case of John Ogilvie, Sprague says he 'can find no account of his going to England for Orders.' He will be found here as returning July 12, 1749.

In order that this book can be readily consulted, it has been arranged alphabetically, although it has not been thought necessary to repeat the word minister after each entry; but in every case where the passenger was a schoolmaster this has been stated, and without doubt they would be in Holy Orders.

One or two others, neither ministers nor schoolmasters, are to be found in this list; they being buried away in the Money Books, it was thought best to include them.

The number of emigrants to be found here is over 1,200. It has been considered desirable to append some account of the first Anglican priests settled in the New World.

<small>First Ministers in Virginia.</small> The history of the settlement of ministers of the Church of England in the North American colonies seems to commence with Virginia, whither Robert Hunt, A.M., on Friday, December 19, 1606, sailed in an expedition from Blackwall. He migrated as a missionary to Virginia from the Primate of all England. This missionary's home appears to have been in Kent, and prior to this mission he was doubtless the Vicar of Reculver, whose appointment to that cure was dated January 18, 1594. His resignation took place in 1602, at which time he appears associated with Gosnold, Smith, and Wingfield, in plans for the settlement of Virginia. The date of his death is unknown.[1]

From the first the ministers could not keep pace with the increase of population, for Perry says, 'Messrs. Whitaker, Stockham, Mease, Bargrave, and Wickham were unable to render the services required by the rapidly-extending colonists.' The number of boroughs was now eleven. Services and Sacraments were in danger of a widespread neglect, and, in this extremity, the Virginia Company sought the aid of the Bishop of London in supplying the colony 'with pious, learned, and painful ministers.' Bishop King, who then filled the see, had already shown his personal interest in the Christianizing of Virginia and in the establishment of the college for the Indians. The Bishop had been chosen a member of the King's Council for Virginia; it was but natural that in all matters ecclesiastical his opinions should have great weight, and there grew out of this personal interest and episcopal care the recognition of the

---

[1] Perry, 'American Episcopal Church,' vol. i., p. 42.

spiritual jurisdiction of the Bishop of London over the colonies which existed, almost without question, until the issue of the War of Independence secured the ecclesiastical as well as the civil independence of the United States.[1]

An early list of the clergy of Virginia is to be found in 'Lists of the Livinge and Dead in Virginia, Feby. 16, 1623,' published by the State of Virginia, 1874; another list is to be found in Neill, ' Notes on the Virginia Colonial Clergy.'

The first visitor to New England in Holy Orders was the Rev. William Morell, who came over in 1623 with Robert Gorges, but saw no opportunity to exercise his ministry, and returned to England.[2]

Early Ministers in New England.

The Church in Maryland was ministered to by the Rev. Richard James, who embarked for Virginia in 1635. Years passed, and in the re-establishment of the monarchy and the restoration of the authority of the Proprietary, we find but little mention of the Church, though the records inform us that about the year 1650 the Rev. William Wilkinson, clerk, fifty years of age, with his wife and family and servants, arrived in the colony. It would seem that Mr. Wilkinson was the first resident clergyman of the Church in the province other than the ministers of Kent Island.

At length there appears to have been in the colony, in the year 1675, three clergymen of the Church of England.[3] In 1681 an allowance was made from the King's Secret Service Fund for the payment of the cost of passage of Rev. Jonathan Sanders to Maryland, and there is among the records of the State Papers Office a recommendation of the Rev. Ambrose Sanderson by the Privy Council, dated October 8, 1681, as a suitable minister for Maryland, while, two years later, the Rev. Duell Pead and the Rev. William Mullett were designated for service in the province.[4] On September 29, 1695, a Secret Service grant was made to defray the passage of Rev. Paul Betrand to Maryland.[5]

In June, 1691, King William complied with the popular wish, and Maryland was constituted a royal colony. The following year, on the arrival of the royal Governor, Sir Lionel Copley, the Crown was finally recognised as the sole source of authority, and the Protestant religion was established.[6] In April, 1696, the Bishop of London offered the appointment of Commissary to Dr. Bray, who accepted, and spared neither labour nor time in securing mission-priests. Through his exertions the number

---

[1] Perry, 'American Episcopal Church,' vol. i., p. 74. [2] *Ibid.*, vol. i., p. 81.
[3] *Ibid.*, vol. i., p. 134. [4] *Ibid.*, vol i., p. 135. [5] *Ibid.*, vol. i., p. 136.
[6] *Ibid.*, vol. i., p. 137.

of the clergy was increased to sixteen ere he set foot upon the soil of Maryland.¹

Beginning of the Ministry in New York and the Middle Colonies.

At the conquest of this colony by the English, under Colonel Richard Nicolls, in 1664, the Church of England service was introduced; and as there was no place of worship but the Dutch Church within the fort, it was cordially arranged by the articles of capitulation that, after the Dutch had finished their use of the building, the chaplain of the British forces should have the occupancy of the same. 'This,' says Brodhead,² 'was all the footing that the English Church had in New York for more than thirty years.' In the ship which brought Governor Andros from England, there came a clergyman who had both Dutch and English Orders—Domine Nicolaus Van Rensselaer.³ In 1677 he was deposed from his ministry on account of his bad life, and the year following he died.⁴ In 1678 the Rev. Charles Wolley came with Governor Andros to New York; he had license to return to England in 1680.⁵ Two years elapsed before the vacant chaplaincy was filled, when Dr. John Gordon was appointed; he remained but a short time, and, on his return, the Rev. Josias Clarke became chaplain. The Rev. Alexander Innes succeeded Mr. Clarke as chaplain of the garrison, and his commission is dated April 20, 1686.⁶

The first minister of Trinity Church, New York, was the Rev. William Vesey, who went to England in 1697 to receive Holy Orders.

Ministry in New Jersey.

In the year 1700 Colonel Lewis Morris sent a memorial to the authorities at home as to the state of religion in the Jerseys, and expressed a wish for the ministry of the famous ex-Quaker, Keith, who held his first service at Amboy, October 4, 1702. In connection with the services of Keith is to be noted the labours of Rev. Alexander Innes and the Rev. John Talbot, who became the apostle of the New Jersey Church.⁷

Boston.

On Saturday, May 15, 1686, the *Rose* frigate entered Boston, bearing the Rev. Robert Ratcliffe, M.A., to whom had been assigned the task of inaugurating the services of the Church in Boston. According to Foster, 'he was the son of Rich, of Broad Clist, Devon; matriculated, 1674; aged 17.⁸ The next minister at Boston was the Rev. Samuel Myles, June 30, 1689, he having been to England for ordination in 1687.

A slight attempt has been made to annotate the information

---

¹ 'American Episcopal Church,' vol. i., p. 138.
² Brodhead's 'History of New York,' vol. i., p. 762.
³ 'History of the Episcopal Church,' vol. i., p. 149.
⁴ *Ibid.*, vol. i., p. 150.   ⁵ *Ibid.*, vol. i., p. 152.   ⁶ *Ibid.*, vol. i., p. 155.
⁷ *Ibid.*, vol. i., p. 166.   ⁸ 'Alumni Oxonienses.'

given in the Treasury record; but, except in scarce names, great difficulty was found in identification. The chief work consulted has been Foster's 'Alumni Oxoniensis,' and many of the ministers have no doubt been placed as graduates of that University; but this must not be taken for granted without corroboration from other sources, nor should a search in Foster be neglected, as in cases of two or three of the same Christian and surname matriculating within a year or so of one another, it was thought best not to attempt identification; also, if the emigrant had a distinctive name, such as Bolton Simpson, who received the £20 in 1745, Foster is worth searching, for he gives a clue to a certain family in this entry: 'Bolton Simpson, son of John, of Redmayne, Cumberland, D.D., 1759; Vicar of W. Cowes, 1744; died 1786.' Another example of relationship between an emigrant and a graduate is Lee Massey, who went to Virginia in 1766; Foster gives 'Leigh Massey, son of James, of Oxmantown, near Dublin, Ireland; matric., 1718; aged 18.'

The reports of the Society for the Propagation of the Gospel contain a vast amount of information as to ordinations, removals from one colony or town to another, parentage, death, return to England, origin, education, previous appointment, date of appointment, former residence. The following are instances:

'Appointment of Mr. Hughes, Chaplain to the 44th Regt. of Foot, formerly of the Diocese of Waterford, Ireland, to the Mission of Amboy in New Jersey.'—S.P.G. Report, 1759, p. 64.

'Removal of Rev. Mr. Carter (who was educated upon the foundation of Eaton School, and afterwards at Peterhouse, Cambridge) from Bahama Islands to Amboy.'—1760, p. 64.

'Mr. Houden is of French extraction.'—1760, p. 53.

'Death of Mr. Clement Hall, a native of England, but who went over to North Carolina and settled in Penquiman's Country, and was put in the Commission of the Peace, but in 1743 tooke Holy Orders, died Jany., 1759, leaving wife and six children.'—1760, p. 57.

'Rev. Mr. Clarke, Rector of S. Philip in Charles Town, he having quitted that station and returned to England.'—1760, p. 61.

'Rev. Mr. Inmer, a Swiss Clergyman, Missionary to Purrysberg in S. Carolina.'—1760, p. 63.

'Mr. Duncanson, educated at Trinity College, Dublin, appointed to the Bahama Islands upon the recommendation of the Bishop of Limerick.'—1761, p. 63.

'Appointment of Rev. Mr. Fayerweather, a native of New England, missionary to the Church of Narraganset. He came to England for Orders, 1756.'—1759, p. 54.

'Rev. Mr. Leaming, catechist at Newport in Rhode Island, to remove to Norwalk.'—1759, p. 54.

'Mr. Usher, the son of the Rev. Mr. Usher, the Society's Missionary at Bristol in New England, who was taken prisoner by the French on his passage to England in the year 1757, and confined in the Castle of Bayonne, in which he died of the Small Pox.'—1759, p. 56.

Amongst the more eminent names of the ministers who received the bounty are Goronwy Owen, premier poet of Wales; Dr. Cutler, Rector of Yale; Robert Stanser, Bishop of Nova Scotia; William White, first American Bishop of the English line; Dr. Charles Inglis, Bishop of Nova Scotia, appointed August 12, 1787, and first Colonial Bishop of the Church of England (Sprague). Dr. Inglis was grandfather of Sir J. E. W. Inglis, the defender of Lucknow ('Dictionary National Biography'); George Keith, first missionary to America of the Society for Propagating the Gospel, and formerly a Quaker; Charles Pittigrew may be mentioned as in the last ship that sailed before the war; Right Rev. Dr. Samuel Seabury, first Bishop of Connecticut; Robert Smith, Bishop of S. Carolina; and Aaron Cleveland, ancestor of President Grover Cleveland.

HOW PEDIGREES ARE TRACED

The compiler takes this opportunity to briefly give a few hints as to the best way of connecting the first ancestor settled in America with his forebears at home.

Every scrap of information that can be obtained in America about the original emigrant should be carefully noted, such as his age, names of children, wife, brothers, sisters, and other relations. When everything has been collected it is time to turn to England for information.

The records of England are vast in extent, badly arranged, scattered about in hundreds of towns and villages, and difficult to understand because of the many different hands and styles in which they are written, the system of contractions and the low Latin used; it is the writer's opinion that the notes taken during the first year's research cannot be depended on, and the work should be checked again from the originals. Having warned the reader against the difficulties of record-searching, we feel constrained to say a few words about people who, without experience, offer their services as searchers.

Many times have we been asked to give a reading of some sentence or word thought to be difficult, and, on examination, the sentence or word has presented no obstacle to anyone versed in such matters. Some of the searchers who offer their services by advertisement are never seen at any search-room, so that, if any research work is done, it must be farmed out amongst others.

Investigations in this country should be commenced with the wills proved in the Prerogative Court of Canterbury (P.C.C.). These have calendars (indices) alphabetical only to the first letter of the name. A list of the wills and administrations for the surname desired has then to be made; on the quantity of wills found depends the question, can every will of the family be read and short abstracts made? If, by reason of their bulk, this cannot be done, some principle of selection must be resorted to, but it is highly desirable that every will should be abstracted; the results of the gleanings in the Prerogative Court of Canterbury should be tabulated and compared with the family notes.

If this Court does not yield the desired knowledge, it will at least point out what part of England the name comes from; in that case the wills proved in the District Registry must be gone into in the same way as the Prerogative Court of Canterbury was done. If a clue is obtained from this source, the parish registers of baptisms, marriages, and burials for the district can be searched.

After this amount of research sufficient material to make a clear pedigree ought to have come to light, but in case this is not so, the contents of that storehouse of records, the Public Record Office, are open to us. The class most easily worked are the Chancery Pleadings.

The compiler has a collection of some 5,000 notes showing the connection between the families of England and America, the result of many years' research and correspondence.

GERALD FOTTERGILL.

11, BRUSSELS ROAD,
  NEW WANDSWORTH,
    LONDON, ENGLAND.

THE LIST

Acourt, John, clerk, Barbadoes, December 28, 1715.—Money Book, 24-193.
Adams, Alexander, Maryland, August 27, 1703.—Money Book, 16-422.
Adams, Alexander, Maryland, January 24, 1748-1749.—Money Book, 43-73.
Adams, James, clerk, North Carolina, July 26, 1707.—Money Book, 19-86.
Addison, Robert, Niagara in Canada, June 24, 1791.—Money Book, 60-91.
Agnew, Andrew, Virginia, July 1, 1709.—Money Book, 20-51.
Agnew, Andrew, clerk, Jamaica, February 7, 1706-1707.—Money Book, 18-405.
Agnew, John, Virginia, June 27, 1753.—Money Book, 44-33.
Airey, Thomas, Maryland, January 24, 1725-1726.—Money Book, 32-145.
Alcock, William, Jamaica, August 17, 1743.—Money Book, 41-4.
Alcock, —, Jamaica, August 10, 1743.—Treasury Minute Book, 29-306-311.
Alexander, John, Georgia, May 1, 1766.—Money Book, 50-2.
Allen, Bennet, Maryland, October 2, 1766.—Money Book, 50-234. Son of James, of Yazor, co. Heref., clerk; M.A., 1760 (Foster).
Allen, Thomas, Leeward Islands, March 16, 1720-1721.—Money Book, 28-34. Son of Benjamin, of Stoke, Staffs; B.A., 1720 (Foster).
Allen, Thomas, clerk, Antigua, December 22, 1711.—Money Book, 21-388.
Allen, Mr., Barbadoes, December 10, 1695.—Money Book, 13-43.
Allett, Thomas, Virginia, April 8, 1718.—Money Book, 26-159.
Allinson, Thomas, his former intended passage to Barbadoes, February 11, 1791.—Money Book, 60-91.
Als, William, Barbadoes, January 6, 1802.—Money Book, 63-15.

Emigrant Ministers to America 11

Alsop, —, clerk, Jamaica, February 3, 1701.—Money Book, 16-17.
Anderson, John, Leeward Islands, February 28, 1717-1718.—Money Book, 27-48.
Andrewes, John, Pennsylvania, February 24, 1767.—Money Book, 50-234. Born near the head of Elk, Cecil Co.; md. April 4, 1746; died Philadelphia, March 29, 1813; Principal of Philadelphia Episcopal Academy (Drake).
Andrews, —, clerk, Virginia, September 13, 1700.—Money Book, 15-154.
Andrews, John, South Carolina, August 8, 1753.—Money Book, 44-33.
Andrews, John, Virginia, April 17, 1749.—Money Book, 43-73.
Andrews, Robert, Virginia, January 19, 1773.—Money Book, 52-41.
Andrews, Samuel, New England, October 8, 1761.—Money Book, 48-155.
Anglin, Philip, Jamaica, November 26, 1776.—Money Book, 53-172.
Anwyl, William, Nova Scotia, May 4, 1749.—Money Book, 43-73.
Arbuthnot, James, clerk, Leeward Islands, October 18, 1705.—Money Book, 18-50.
Arnold, Jonathan, New England, March 19, 1735-1736.—Money Book, 38-267. M.A., 1735-1736 (Foster).
Arrowsmith, —, Maryland, Schoolmaster and Chaplain, January 18, 1695-1696.—Money Book, 13-63.
Atkin, Thomas, Maryland, March 3, 1766.—Money Book, 50-52.
Atkins, Robert, Jamaica, August 8, 1753.—Money Book, 44-33.
Auchmuty, Samuel, New York, July 30, 1747.—Money Book, 42-52. Born Boston, Mass., January 16, 1722; died New York, March 6, 1777; son of Robert, of Boston, an eminent lawyer (Drake).
Austin, Hugh Williams, Barbadoes, August 31, 1779.—Money Book, 54-105. He had a son, Hugh William, of Barbadoes; matriculated 1811 (Foster).
Austin, Richard, Barbadoes, March 31, 1795.—Money Book, 61-42.
Avery, Ephraim, New York, June 3, 1766.—Money Book, 49-306.
Avery, Isaac, Virginia, November 9, 1769.—Money Book, 51-249.
Avon, Archibald, Virginia, February 10, 1767.—Money Book, 50-234.

Ayres, William, New Jersey, January 12, 1766.—Money Book, 50-233.
Babcock, Luke, New England, February 20, 1770.—Money Book, 51-249. Son of Chief Justice Babcock, of Rhode Island (Drake).
Backhouse, Richard, Pennsylvania, August 20, 1728.—Money Book, 34-189.
Badger, Moses, New Hampshire, February 27, 1767.—Money Book, 50-234.
Bagge, John, Virginia, November 13, 1717.—Money Book, 26-101.
Bagger, Mathias, Jamaica, May 10, 1727.—Money Book, 33-307.
Bailey, Jacob, New England, March 18, 1760.—Money Book, 47-108. Born Rowley, Ms., April 16, 1731; died Annapolis, N.J., July 26, 1808.
Bailie, Andrew, clerk, Barbadoes, October 28, 1709.—Money Book, 20-172.
Baily, Thomas, clerk, Naraganzett, March 27, 1712.—Money Book, 21-470.
Baker, Thomas, Virginia, September 8, 1769.—Money Book, 51-249.
Balfour, James, Newfoundland, July 11, 1764.—Money Book, 49-306.
Balfour, William, Virginia, January 23, 1738-1739.—Money Book, 39-17.
Ball, Thomas, Carolina, schoolmaster, March 19, 1725-1726.—Money Book, 32-145. Son of Laurence, of Eccleston, Lancs; B.A. 1719 (Foster).
Balmain, Alexander, Virginia, October 20, 1772.—Money Book, 52-40.
Balneavis, William, Antigua, October 30, 1712.—Money Book, 22-89.
Barclay, Henry, Virginia, December 5, 1737.—Money Book, 39-17. Joint translator of the Liturgy into Mohawk. Rector of Trinity, New York; died August 20, 1764 (Sprague).
Barclay, Thomas, clerk, New York, June 4, 1707.—Money Book, 18-476.
Barclay, William, clerk, New England, November 30, 1703.—Money Book, 17-23.
Barker, James, St. John's, October 19, 1780.—Money Book, 55-115.
Barlow, Henry, Virginia, June 4, 1725.—Money Book, 32-4.
Barnett, John, North Carolina, May 10, 1765.—Money Book, 49-306.

Baron, —, clerk, Maryland, March 14, 1700-1701.—Money Book, 15-259.
Baron, Robert, Bermudas, January 15, 1700-1701.—Money Book, 15-233.
Baron, Robert, Maryland, June 27, 1714.—Money Book, 23-159.
Baron, Robert, South Carolina, February 14, 1753.—Money Book, 44-33
Barret, Robert, Virginia, December 5, 1737.—Money Book, 39-17.
Barrett, John, Virginia (notwithstanding a like sum has been paid before for his passage to Maryland, but happened to be cast away off the Isle of Wight in December last), March 3, 1723-1724.—Money Book, 31-51.
Barrett, John, Maryland, July 29, 1723.—Money Book, 30-78.
Barrol, William, Maryland, March 18, 1760.—Money Book, 47-108.
Barrow, —, clerk, Virginia, August 11, 1702.—Money Book, 16-68. Treasury Papers give John, and Connecticut, vols. lxxx-xciv.
Barton, John, Jamaica, March 14, 1794.—Money Book, 61-42. Son of Newton, of Langley, Berks, M.A., 1784 (Foster).
Barton, Thomas, Pennsylvania, February 7, 1755.—Money Book, 45-111. Born in Ireland, 1730; Trinity College, Dublin (Sprague).
Bass, Edward, New England, June 10, 1752.—Money Book, 44-33. First Bishop of Massachusetts; born Dorchester, November 23, 1726; died September 10, 1803 (Drake).
Bastock, —, clerk, Virginia, July 17, 1700.—Money Book, 15-154.
Batwill, Daniel, His Majesty's Dominions in North America, October 26, 1773.—Money Book, 52-41.
Beach, Abraham, New Jersey, June 23, 1767.—Money Book, 50-234. Born Cheshire, Connecticut, September 9, 1740; died September 11, 1828 ; Rector of New Brunswick, New Jersey (Drake).
Beckett, Thomas, Virginia, May 10, 1727.—Money Book, 35-307.
Beckett, William, Pennsylvania, March 25, 1721.—Money Book, 28-34.
Beechin, James, Maryland, December 10, 1695.—Money Book, 13-43.
Bell, John, Virginia, January 21, 1711-1712.—Money Book, 21-419.
Bennett, Joseph, Nova Scotia, March 24, 1762.—Money Book, 48-155.

Beresford, John, Leeward Islands, June 27, 1714.—Money Book, 23-159.
Beresford, Samuel, clerk, Barbadoes, October 11, 1700.—Money Book, 15-185.
Berisford, Samuel, clerk, Barbadoes, March 15, 1711-1712.—Money Book, 21-459.
Beronville, John, Leeward Islands, May 30, 1733.—Money Book, 37-37.
Berry, Jeremiah, Maryland, January 19, 1769.—Money Book, 51-79.
Betham, Rev. Robert, Charles Town, in South Carolina, October 16, 1745.—Exchequer of Receipt, vol. 407. Son of Robert, of Woodfoot, Westmorland; M.A. 1742 (Foster).
Betham, Robert, South Carolina, October 22, 1745.—Money Book, 42-52.
Betham, —, clerk, Maryland, September 18, 1700.—Money Book, 15-175.
Betty, John, Virginia, February 27, 1732-1733.—Money Book, 36-480.
Bever, Richard, schoolmaster, South Carolina, January 16, 1711-1712.—Money Book, 21-419.
Beys, —, clerk, New York, February 2, 1709-1710.—Money Book, 20-223.
Bickford, Nathaniel, clerk, Antegoa, June 3, 1713.—Money Book, 22-241.
Bishop, —, Jamaica, November 17, 1720.—Money Book, 28-325.
Bisset, George, Rhode Island, May 12, 1767.—Money Book, 50-234.
Bissett, George, St. John's, April 9, 1786.—Money Book, 58-53.
Bitton, John, Maryland, schoolmaster, March 21, 1706-1707.—Money Book, 18-430.
Black, William, clerk, one of the Jerseys, September 5, 1706.—Money Book, 18-285.
Blackamore, Arthur, Virginia, schoolmaster, September 26, 1707.—Money Book, 19-87.
Blackburn, Benjamin, Bermuda, January 7, 1774.—Money Book, 52-41.
Blacknall, John, North Carolina, June 7, 1725.—Money Book, 32-4.
Blackwell, Robert, Virginia, June 18, 1772.—Money Book, 52-40.
Blagrove, Benjamin, Virginia, March 10, 1772.—Money Book, 52-40. Son of John, of Oxford; matriculated 1764 (Foster).

Blair, John, clerk, North Carolina, April 17, 1703.—Money Book, 16-284.
Blair, John, clerk, West Indies, December 7, 1702.—Money Book, 17-287.
Blair, William, Monserat, October 18, 1750.—Money Book, 43-419.
Bland, William, Virginia, July 15, 1767.—Money Book, 50-234.
Blenman, Rev. T., Barbadoes, June 27, 1783.—Money Book, 56-249. Son of Jonath, of Bridge Town, Barbadoes, Arm; matriculated 1741.
Blin, Peter, North Carolina, October 5, 1769.—Money Book, 51-249.
Blomfield, Joseph, Virginia, July 3, 1735.—Money Book, 38-33.
Bloomer, Joshua, New York, March 2, 1769.—Money Book, 51-79.
Blount, Nathaniel, North Carolina, August 27, 1773.—Money Book, 52-41.
Boardman, —, Leeward Islands, May 7, 1701.—Money Book, 15-408.
Boardslee, John, New England, October 8, 1761.—Money Book, 48-155.
Bonneval, Rev. Lewis de, Jamaica, January 23, 1738-1739.—Money Book, 39-17.
Booths, Charles, South Carolina, January 10, 1744-1745.—Money Book, 41-4.
Borrowdale, William, Nevis, July 11, 1815 (1805 ?).—Money Book, 63-15.
Boschi, Charles, South Carolina, December 20, 1744.—Treasury Minute Book, 30-104-5.
Bosomnworth, Rev. Thomas, Georgia, July 4, 1743.—Exchequer of Receipt, vol. 407.
Bosomworth, Thomas, Georgia, July 6, 1743.—Treasury Minute Book, 29-289-92. Money Book, 41-4.
Bostwick, Gideon, Massachusetts Bay, March 22, 1770.—Money Book, 51-249. Son of Nathaniel and Esther (Hitchcock) Bostwick. Born at North Milford, September 21, 1742 (Sprague).
Boucker, Henry, Maryland, January 11, 1697-1698.—Money Book, 15-424.
Boucher, Jonathan, Virginia, March 30, 1762.—Money Book, 48-272. Born at Blencogo, Cumberland, England, March 12, 1738 (Sprague).
Bouire, John, Maryland, January 19, 1773.—Money Book, 52-41.
Bowcher, Robert, Barbadoes, January 18, 1757.—Money Book,

46-62. Son of Robert, of Barbadoes; matriculated 1752 (Foster).
Bowcher, Clement, Barbadoes, October 9, 1790.—Money Book, 60-92.
Bowdler, George, Granada, September 13, 1764.—Money Book, 49-306. Son of George, of Shrewsbury, Salop; M.A. 1752 (Foster).
Bowen, John, Antigua, January 9, 1760.—Money Book, 47-108. Son of George, of Wolfsdale, co. Pèmbroke, clerk; B.A. 1753 (Foster).
Boyd, Andrew, Virginia, July 1, 1709.—Money Book, 20-51.
Brace, Edward, schoolmaster, Barbadoes, January 16, 1711-1712.—Money Book, 21-419.
Brace, Edward, Barbadoes, January 10, 1750-1751.—Money Book, 43-419.
Brachen, John, Virginia, July 28, 1772.—Money Book, 52-40. President of William and Mary College in 1813; died Williamsburg, Virginia, July 15, 1818 (Drake).
Bradshaw, Thomas, St. Vincent, March 31, 1778.—Money Book, 54-106.
Braidfoot, John, Virginia, April 28, 1772.—Money Book, 52-40.
Braithwaite, Thomas, Maryland, January 22, 1776.—Money Book, 53-172.
Braithwaite, Robert, Barbadoes, October 9, 1750.—Money Book, 43-419.
Brandler, John, Virginia, March 14, 1759.—Money Book, 46-62.
Brett, —, clerk, Carolina, June 7, 1700.—Money Book, 15-120.
Breynton, John, Nova Scotia, May 6, 1752.—Money Book, 44-33. D.D. 1770 (Foster).
Briggs, Robert, North Carolina, April 14, 1768.—Money Book, 30-492.
Brisac, —, clerk, New York, January 29, 1700-1701.—Money Book, 15-248.
Brochin, James, Virginia (he having been taken by the French in his former voyage to that place), November 16, 1702.—Money Book, 16-189.
Brockwell, Charles, New England, May 12, 1737.—Money Book, 39-17.
Brody, —, Virginia, June 25, 1709.—Money Book, 20-44.
Brogden, William, Virginia, September 11, 1735.—Money Book, 38-33. Son of William Brogden, of Calvert Co., Md. (Sprague).
Brook, Zacharias, Virginia, July 24, 1719.—Money Book, 27-325.

Brooke, Clement, South Carolina, February 7, 1775.—Money Book, 45-111.
Brookes, John, clerk, Jerzies, March 27, 1705.—Money Book, 17-344.
Brown, James, St. Vincent, March 23, 1779.—Money Book, 54-106.
Brown, James, St. Vincent, June 28, 1779.—Money Book, 54-106.
Brown, William, clerk, schoolmaster, Barbaodes, March 30, 1715.—Money Book, 23-515.
Brown, Isaac, New York, September 1, 1733.—Money Book, 37-37.
Brown, Richard, Maryland, July 18, 1750.—Money Book, 43-419.
Brown, Arthur, Providence in New England, November 12, 1729.—Money Book, 35-31. Son of Rev. John B. Brown. Born 1699, at Drogheda, Ireland (Sprague).
Brown, Thomas, North America, August 20, 1764.—Money Book, 49-306.
Browne, James, Providence in the Bahama Islands, April 10, 1784.—Money Book, 57-78.
Bruce, John, Virginia, March 7, 1775.—Money Book, 53-172.
Bruen, —, Leeward Islands, October 10, 1710.—Money Book, 20-397.
Brunkell, John, Virginia, May 6, 1715.—Money Book, 23-555.
Bruskill, John, Virginia, October 11, 1752.—Money Book, 44-33.
Bryzoluis, Paulus, Nova Scotia, March 3, 1767.—Money Book, 50-234.
Buchan, Robert, Virginia, March 20, 1772.—Money Book, 52-40.
Buchanan, John, Virginia, September 5, 1775.—Money Book, 53-172. Born at Dumfries, Scotland, in 1748 (Sprague).
Buchanan, Mathew, clerk, Carolina, July 21, 1710.—Money Book, 20-328.
Buchanan, Mathew, New York, August 7, 1704.—Money Book, 17-194.
Buckham, William, Virginia, April 22, 1763 (?).—Money Book, 48-272.
Bull, William Tredwell, clerk, South Carolina, July 1, 1712.—Money Book, 21-551.
Bull, William, Carolina, November 17, 1719.—Money Book, 27-284.
Burger, Peter Christian, Nova Scotia, January 20, 1752.—Money Book, 44-33.

Burges, Thomas, North Carolina, October 2, 1741.—Money Book, 40-20.
Burges, Colin, Jamaica, June 2, 1796.—Money Book, 61-42.
Burges, Henry John, North Carolina, November 11, 1768.—Money Book, 51-79.
Burnett, —, clerk, Virginia, September 18, 1700.—Money Book, 15-175.
Burrough, Phillip, clerk, Maryland, March 12, 1710-1711.—Money Book, 21-32.
Butler, Edward, Virginia, February 3, 1704-1705.—Money Book, 17-287.
Byam, Henry, Antigua, November 20, 1754.—Money Book, 45-111.
Byam, Francis, Antigua, September 1, 1733.—Money Book, 37-37.
Byles, Mather, New England, June 30, 1768.—Money Book, 51-79. Son of Mather Byles, Rector of Christ Church, Boston; born January 12, 1735; died March 12, 1814 (Drake); D.D. 1770 (Foster).

Caddell, Henry, Barbadoes, November 20, 1798.—Money Book, 62-188.
Cairon, John, Virginia, October 10, 1710.—Money Book, 20-397.
Camp, Icabod, New England, April 7, 1752.—Money Book, 44-33.
Camp, Michael, South Carolina, April 16, 1752.—Money Book, 44-33.
Campbell, James, Virginia, January 17, 1721-1722.—Money Book, 29-203.
Campbell, Alexander, Jamaica, September 10, 1803.—Money Book, 63-15.
Campbell, John, Jamaica, November 21, 1780.—Money Book, 55-115.
Campbell, John, Virginia, June 11, 1773.—Money Book, 52-41.
Campbell, Colin, Jamaica, October 9, 1751.—Money Book, 44-33.
Campbell, Isaac, Virginia, July 13, 1747.—Money Book, 42-52.
Campbell, Archibald, Virginia, February 4, 1745-1746.—Money Book, 42-52.
Campbell, Alexander, Virginia, December 30 1725.—Money Book, 32-145.
Campbell, Colin, Isle of Nevis, February 9, 1737-1738.—Order Book, 16-397.
Cancellar, Stephen, clerk, Antegoa, January 31, 1710-1711.—Money-Book, 21-9.

Emigrant Ministers to America 19

Caner, Henry, New England, September 14, 1727.—Money Book, 33-333. Son of Henry and Abigail Caner (Sprague); M.A. 1735 (Foster).

Caner, Richard, Connecticut, February 4, 1741-1742.—Money Book, 40-20.

Cant, —, Leeward Islands, June 29, 1692.—Money Book, 11-347. King's Warrant Book, 9-272.

Carew, Walter, Jamaica, October 19, 1780.—Money Book, 55-115.

Cargill, John, Leeward Islands, April 21, 1708.—Money Book, 19-244.

Carter, Jessie, Virginia, November 3, 1772.—Money Book, 52-40.

Carter, Robert, New Providence in Bahama Islands, September 27, 1749.—Money Book, 43-73. Son of William Carter, of Kimmel, Flint. M.A. 1747 (Foster).

Caulfield, John, Island of St. John's, August 25, 1769.—Money Book, 51-249.

Cawthren, William, Virginia, December 30, 1725.—Money Book, 32-145.

Chabrand, David, Canada, April 19, 1766. — Money Book, 50-2.

Chandler, Thomas Bradbury, New Jersey, September 4, 1751. —Money Book, 44-33. Son of William and Jemima (Bradbury) Chandler. Born at Woodstock, April 26, 1726 (Sprague). D.D. 1766 (Foster).

Chapman, George, Pensacola, May 12, 1773 —Money Book, 52-41.

Chapman, John, Virginia, April 10, 1719.—Money Book, 27-153.

Chapple, Jonathan, Bermuda, July 27, 1743.—Money Book, 41-4. Son of Jonathan Chapple, of Cleyhidon, Devon. Matriculated 1732 (Foster).

Charlton, Richard C., B.A., Leeward Islands, April 4, 1730. Treasury Board Papers, vol. 273, 41a. Warrant dated April 15, 1730.—Money Book, 35-89.

Chase, Thomas, Maryland, February 21, 1738-1739. —Money Book, 39-380.

Checkley, —, New England, June 21, 1738.—Order Book, 16-338. John, born Boston, 1680 (Sprague). M.A. 1738 (Foster).

Chichley, William, Virginia, September 24, 1729.—Money Book, 34-506.

Christian, Nicholas, North Carolina, August 27, 1773.—Money Book, 52-41.

Clack, Mr., Maryland, December 10, 1695.—Money Book, 13-43.

Clagett, Thomas John, Maryland, October 23, 1767.—Money Book, 50-234. Born in Prince George's County. Md., October 2, 1743. Son of Rev. Samuel Clagett. Bishop of Maryland 1792. Died August 2, 1816 (Sprague).

Clare, George, Jamaica, March 27, 1712.—Money Book, 21-470.

Clark, William, New England, February 7, 1769.—Money Book, 51-79.

Clark, John, Antegoa, December 13, 1723.—Money Book, 30-168.

Clark, Timothy, Jamaica, January 17, 1786.—Money Book, 58-53.

Clark, James, Antigua, September, 26, 1787.—Money Book, 58-441.

Clark, Moses, New England, November 17, 1720.—Money Book, 28-325.

Clarke, William, Jamaica, January 7, 1766 or 1768.—Money Book, 50-234.

Clarke, Richard, South Carolina, August 15, 1753.—Money Book, 44-33. Born in England (Sprague).

Clarke, Richard, Connecticut, March 3, 1767.—Money Book, 50-234.

Clay, Charles, Virginia, June 8, 1769.—Money Book, 51-249.

Clayton, Thomas, Maryland, January 11, 1697-1698.—Money Book, 13-424.

Cleater, Joseph, clerk, schoolmaster, New York, July 9, 1706.—Money Book, 18-254.

Clephane, David, Virginia, March 28, 1710.—Money Book, 20-241.

Clerk, Andrew, schoolmaster, New York, May 2, 1705.—Money Book, 17-364.

Cleveland, Aaron, Pennsylvania, July 30, 1755.—Money Book, 45-111. Born Cambridge, Massachusetts, October 19, 1715. Son of Aaron and Abigail (Waters) Cleveland. Died August 11, 1757 (Sprague).

Clinch, John, Trinity Bay, Newfoundland, March 12, 1787.—Money Book, 57-53.

Clubb, John, clerk, Pennsylvania, April 3, 1704.—Money Book, 17-108.

Cockburn, Alexander, Leeward Islands, October 10, 1710.—Money Book, 20-397.

Colbatch, Joseph, Maryland, January 11, 1697-1698.—Money Book, 13-424.

Colby, Samuel, Jamaica, December 10, 1709.—Money Book, 20-191.

Cole, Samuel, Newfoundland, June 6, 1792.—Money Book, 60-

Emigrant Ministers to America 21

91. Son of William Cole, of Portsea, Hants. Matriculated 1787 (Foster).
Cole, Roscow, Virginia, February 21, 1748-1749. Money Book, 43-73.
Colgan, Thomas, New York, June 2, 1726.—Money Book, 32-145.
Colladon, David, South Carolina, April 6, 1733.—Money Book, 36-480.
Colleire, —, Maryland, July 28, 1698.—Money Book, 14-171.
Collins, George, Montserat, December 2, 1802.—Money Book, 63-15.
Collins, William, Jamaica, October 3, 1700.—Money Book, 15 185 or 182.
Collins, Henry, Virginia, May 8, 1722.—Money Book, 29-203.
Collinson, Joseph, Virginia, January 9, 1760.—Money Book, 47-108.
Colten, Jonathan, New England, April 7, 1752.—Money Book, 44-33.
Comin, James, schoolmaster, Leeward Islands, May 8, 1695.— Money Book, 12-509.
Cook, George, Maryland, January 24, 1748-1749.—Money Book, 43-73.
Cooke, Samuel, New Jersey, June 6, 1751.—Money Book, 44-33.
Coombe, Thomas, Pennsylvania, October 29, 1771.—Money Book, 52-40.
Cooper, Robert, South Carolina, May 11, 1758.—Money Book, 46-62.
Cooper, Miles, New York, August 11, 1762.—Money Book, 48-272. Son of William Cooper, of Millum, Cumberland. D.C.L. 1767 (Foster).
Cooper, John, clerk, Antegoa, March 29, 1711.—Money Book, 21-47.
Copp, Jonathan, Georgia, February 12, 1750-1751.—Money Book, 43-419.
Cordiner, William, clerk, New England, November 19, 1706.— Money Book, 18-343.
Cosgrove, James, North Carolina, March 3, 1766.—Money Book, 50-2.
Cossit, Ranna, New Hampshire, March 30, 1773.—Money Book, 52-41.
Cotton, Nathaniel, West Florida, March 8, 1768.—Money Book, 50-492.
Coughlan, Lawrence, Newfoundland, May 1, 1766.—Money Book, 50-2.

Coulet, Rev. Stephen, South Carolina, August 3, 1731.—Money Book, vol. 36-84.
Coull, James, Antigua, January 19, 1773.—Money Book, 52-41.
Cowper, John, clerk, Virginia, April 16, 1716.—Money Book, 24-416.
Cox, Charles, Maryland, March 14, 1691-1692.—King's Warrant Book, 9-198. Son of Andrew Cox, of Kemberton, Salop, clerk, 1677 (Foster).
Cox, James, Maryland, June 21, 1723.—Money Book, 30-78.
Cradock, Thomas, Maryland, February 28, 1743-1744.—Money Book, 41-4. Born at Wolverham, Bedfordshire, England, in 1718; died May 7, 1770 (Sprague).
Craig, George, Pennsylvania, September 12, 1750.—Money Book, 43-419.
Craig, James, Virginia, April 4, 1755.—Money Book, 45-111. Son of Philip Craig, of London. B.A. 1746 (Foster).
Craig, James, Virginia, October 11, 1758.—Money Book, 46-62.
Cramp, John, North Carolina, October 9, 1767.—Money Book, 50-234.
Crawford, Thomas, clerk, Maryland, January 18, 1703-1704.—Money Book, 17-62, 306.
Crawford, James, clerk, Maryland, January 8, 1711-1712.—Money Book, 21-408.
Crooke, John Pogson, Leeward Islands, April 1, 1769.—Money Book, 51-249.
Cruden, Alexander, Virginia, March 22, 1749-1750.—Money Book, 43-73.
Crupples, Charles, North Carolina, June 13, 1766.—Money Book, 50-2.
Cuming, John, Grenades, January 4, 1770.—Money Book, 51-249.
Cuming, Robert, North Carolina, January 31, 1748-1749.—Money Book, 43-73.
Cumini, Alexander, Jamaica, August 11, 1785.—Money Book, 57-35.
Cumming, George, clerk, Leeward Islands, April 14, 1709.—Money Book, 19-473.
Cummings, Archibald, Pennsylvania, January 24, 1725-1726.—Money Book, 32-145.
Cuningham, —, clerk, Jamaica, February 27, 1700-1701.—Money Book, 15-259.
Cuningham, —, clerk, Jamaica, October 11, 1700.—Money Book, 15-185.
Cunningham, Charles, clerk, Jamaica, November 7, 1707.—Money Book, 19-112.

Emigrant Ministers to America 23

Curphey, Thomas, Bahama Islands, February 14, 1722-1723.—Money Book, 30-78.
Currie, William, Pennsylvania, October 7, 1736.—Money Book, 38-267.
Curtin, James, Antigua, October 30, 1798.—Money Book, 61-42.
Cutler, Dr. Timothy, New England, June 28, 1723.—Money Book, 30-78. Born Charlestown, Massachusetts, in 1683; died August, 1765. Son of Major John Cutler (Sprague).
Cutler, Thomas, voyage to America 'to make tryall of a rich Silver Mine.' £200 for passage money. June 23, 1698.—King's Warrant Book, 12-515.
Cutting, Leonard, New Jersey, February 9, 1764.—Money Book, 49-182. Born Great Yarmouth, England, 1724; died January 25, 1794.

Daly, Rees, Montserrat, December 18, 1735.—Money Book, 38-33. Son of John Daly, of Montserrat. Arm. Exeter College; matriculated July 13, 1731, aged eighteen (Foster).
Davenport, Jos., Virginia, October 23, 1755.—Money Book, 45-111.
Davenport, Addington, New England, February 27, 1732-1733.—Money Book, 36-480. M.A. 1732-1733. Native of New England. Notes and Queries, 1888.
Davidson, Alexander, Maryland, March 8, 1710-1711.—Money Book, 21-32.
Davies, William, St. Christopher's, January 26, 1791.—Money Book, 60-91.
Davies, Thomas, New England, October 8, 1761.—Money Book, 48-155. Born at Kington, Herefordshire, England, December 21, 1736; died May 12, 1766 (Sprague).
Davis, Charles, clerk, Carbonera, Newfoundland, May 12, 1713.—Money Book, 22-228.
Davis, Thomas, Virginia, October 13, 1773.—Money Book, 32-41.
Davis, Anthony, Jamaica, October 6, 1757.—Money Book, 46-62.
Davis, Thomas, Virginia, September 25, 1754.—Money Book, 45-111.
Davis, Peter, Virginia, June 25, 1751.—Money Book, 44-33.
Davis, Stapleton, Leeward Islands, November 12, 1729.—Money Book, 35-41. Cambridge, B.A. 1721; incorp. Oxford, May 22, 1723 (Foster).
Dawney, Francis, Jamaica, March 22, 1785.—Money Book, 57-35.

Dawson, William, Pensacola, West Florida, July 11, 1764.—Money Book, 49-306. Son of John Dawson, of Burton, Staffordshire, clerk. B.A. 1764.
Dean, Henry, clerk, Barbadoes, July 10, 1695.—Money Book, 12-572.
Deane, Barzillai, New England, November 26, 1745.—Money Book, 42-52.
Debutts, Lawrence, clerk, Virginia, July 9, 1721. Money Book, 29-65.
De La Roche, Peter, Nova Scotia, March 14, 1771.—Money Book, 52-40.
Dell, Thomas, Virginia, June 2, 1721.—Money Book, 29-4.
Dennis, Benjamin, schoolmaster, South Carolina, October 10, 1710.—Money Book, 20-397.
Dent, Samuel, Barbadoes, January 19, 1773.—Money Book, 54-41.
Dety, John, New York, January 8, 1771.—Money Book, 51-249.
Deucher, Alexander, Barbadoes, March 18, 1717-1718.—Money Book, 26-159.
Dibble, Abenezer, America, September 14, 1748.—Money Book, 43-73.
Dick, Archibald, Virginia, March 30, 1762. Money Book, 48-272.
Dick, Rev. Mr. Archibald, Virginia, March 26, 1762.—Exchequer of Receipt, vol. 407.
Dickie, Adam, Virginia, April 12, 1731.—Money Book, 35-89.
Dicks, John, clerk, Jamaica, August 28, 1711.—Money Book, 21-170.
Dixon, Philip, Bermudas, August 16, 1793.—Money Book, 60-91.
Dixon, John, Virginia, September 7, 1748. Money Book, 43-73.
Doide, Townshend, Virginia, August 15, 1765.
Donaldson, John, clerk, Maryland, February 12, 1711-1712.—Money Book, 21-437.
Donaldson, Colin, Jamaica, June 3, 1801.—Money Book, 62-188.
Dotin, John, Barbadoes, February 8, 1796.—Money Book, 61-42.
Doty, John, Sorrell, Canada, February 14, 1784.—Money Book, 57-35.
Douglas, Alexander, South Carolina, September 5, 1750.—Money Book, 43-419.
Douglas, Rev. John, Antigua, November 30, 1732.—Money Book, 36-259.

Emigrant Ministers to America

Douglass, William, Virginia, October 5, 1749. Money Book, 43-73.
Dow, John, Jamaica, January 14, 1728-1729.—Money Book, 34-340.
Dowie, William, Maryland, April 6, 1762.—Money Book, 48-272.
Doyle, Owen, Maryland, October 4, 1711.—Money Book, 21-200.
Drage, Theodorus Swaine, North Carolina, June 8, 1769. —Money Book, 51-249.
Drew, Patrick, Jamaica, October 10, 1710.—Money Book, 20-397.
Duckworth, Mr., Island of S. Christopher's, March 12, 1773. —Money Book, 52-41.
Duke, Rev. J., Barbadoes, June 20, 1783.—Money Book, 56, 249.
Duke, John, Barbadoes, August 31, 1779.—Money Book, 54-105.
Duke, William, Barbadoes, May 24, 1758.—Money Book, 46-62.
Dun, William, clerk, Carolina, December 10, 1705.—Money Book, 18-85.
Dunbar, Hancock, Virginia, December 30, 1725.—Money Book, 32-145.
Duncan, David, Leeward Islands, January 8, 1711-1712.— Money Book, 21-408.
Duncan, Alexander, Carolina, January 28, 1716-1717.—Money Book, 25-195.
Dundass, John, South Carolina, June 11, 1773.—Money Book, 52-41.
Dwight, Daniel, M.A., New England, June 2, 1729.—Treasury Board Papers, vol. 271, 42. Warrant dated June 4, 1729.— Money Book, 34-428. M.A. 1729 (Foster).
Dymocke, James, Jamaica, May 17, 1792.—Money Book, 60-91.

Eager, Thomas, clerk, New England, April 25, 1712.—Money Book, 21-507.
Eagleson, John, Nova Scotia, April 14, 1768.—Money Book, 50-492.
Earle, Daniel, North Carolina, September 23, 1756.—Money Book, 45-111.
Eartwick, William, South Carolina, June 16, 1775.—Money Book, 53-172.
Edmiston, William, Maryland, March 31, 1767.—Money Book, 50-234.
Edwards, John, Barbadoes, January 8, 1750-1751.—Money Book, 43-419.

Edwards, Thomas, clerk, Virginia, November 30, 1702.—Money Book, 16-202.
Edwards, —, Maryland, May 7, 1701.—Money Book, 15-408.
Edwards, Jos., South Carolina, July 21, 1762.—Money Book, 48-272.
Ehl, John James, Minister to the Palatine Colonies in New York, October 5, 1722.—Money Book, 30-21.
Elebech, Henry, Virginia.—Order Book, 16-81, January 11, 1731-1732.
Ellington, Edward, Georgia, May 12, 1767.—Money Book, 50-234.
Ellis, Rowland, schoolmaster to Burlington in New Jersey, November 13, 1711.—Money Book, 21-221.
Emerson, Arthur, Antigua, March 19, 1735-1736.—Money Book, 38-267.
Emilian, —, clerk, Maryland, March 7, 1700-1701.—Money Book, 15-259.
Emmerson, Arthur, Virginia, November 11, 1768.—Money Book, 51-79. Son of John Emmerson, of Newcastle-on-Tyne. B.A. 1733 (Foster).
Erskine, George, clerk, Jamaica, May 1, 1711.—Money Book, 21-72.
Evans, Rev. John, appointed a priest in Newfoundland, January 14, 1791.—Exchequer of Receipt, vol. 407.
Evans, Hugh, Newfoundland, January 26, 1791.—Money Book, 60-91.
Evans, Evan, clerk, Philadelphia, August 9, 1708.—Money Book, 19-335. Native of Wales; will proved November 10, 1721 (Sprague).
Evans, Owen, clerk, Virginia, March 14, 1706-1707.—Money Book, 18-424.
Evans, Jonathan, clerk, Virginia, May 21, 1707.—Money Book, 18-465.
Evans, —, clerk, Pennsylvania, July 5, 1700.—Money Book, 15-143.
Evans, Nathaniel, New Jersey, September 23, 1765.—Money Book, 50-52.
Evans, John, South Carolina, March 24, 1760.—Money Book, 48-155.
Evans, George, Jamaica, January 18, 1749-1750.—Money Book, 43-73.
Eversfield, John, Maryland, September 26, 1727.—Money Book, 33-334. Son of Matthew Eversfield, of Tunbridge, Kent. B.A. 1727 (Foster).
Ewing, Alex, Bermuda, December 12, 1787.—Money Book, 58-441.

Emigrant Ministers to America 27

Faber, Tanaquill, clerk, Virginia, July 20, 1709.—Money Book, 20-77.
Falconar, Patrick, clerk, Virginia, April 29, 1710.—Money Book, 20-265.
Falconer, James, Virginia, October 8, 1718.—Money Book, 27-3.
Fancourt, Thomas, Tobago, September 4, 1799.—Money Book, 62-188.
Fanning, William, North Carolina, March 27, 1754.—Money Book, 45-10.
Farquharson, James, clerk, Pennsylvania, April 25, 1712.—Money Book, 21-507.
Farquharson, Alexander, New Jersey, August 12, 1717.—Money Book, 25-341.
Faux, Mr., Virginia, October 10, 1695.—Money Book, 13-43.
Fayerweather, Samuel, New England, April 14, 1756.—Money Book, 45-111. M.A. 1756 (Foster).
Feilde, Thomas, America, August 16, 1770.—Money Book, 51-249.
Feveryear, John, Bermuda, October 23, 1755 (?).—Money Book, 45-111.
Finch. See Frinh.
Findlater, John, Grenades, June 18, 1771.—Money Book, 52-40.
Findlay, Alexander, Georgia, September 27, 1770.—Money Book, 51-249.
Finnie, Alexander, Virginia, December 17, 1724.—Money Book, 31-341.
Fishe, Samuel, North Carolina, September 12, 1766.—Money Book, 50-2.
Fisher, N., Nova Scotia, October 30, 1777.—Money Book, 53-172. Born Dedham, Massachusetts, July 8, 1742; died December 20, 1820. Rector of St. Peter's, Salem (Sprague).
Fisher, Nathaniel, Nova Scotia, October 30, 1777.—Money Book, 54-106.
Fleming, Thomas, Leeward Islands, June 25, 1730.—Money Book, 35-89.
Fletcher, Thomas, Maryland, July 9, 1721.—Money Book, 29-4.
Fogg, Daniel, Massachusetts Bay, September 3, 1770.—Money Book, 51-249.
Forbes, Robert, clerk, Carolina, March 10, 1707-1708.—Money Book, 19-200.
Forbes, Alexander, clerk, Virginia, February 25, 1709-10.—Money Book, 20-320.

Forbes, John, East Florida, May 10, 1764.—Money Book, 49-182.
Forbes, John, East New Jersey, September 1, 1733.—Money Book, 37-37.
Ford, Hezekiah, North Carolina, October 12, 1776.—Money Book, 53-172.
Fordyce, John, Jamaica, June 2, 1730.—Money Book, 35-89.
Forman, Ric., South Carolina, November 22, 1768.—Money Book, 51-79.
Foster, George, Maryland, January 11, 1697-1698.—Money Book, 13-424.
Fotheringham, William, Newfoundland, June 16, 1762.—Money Book, 48-272.
Foules, James, Virginia, January 24, 1750-1751.—Money Book, 43-419.
Fountaine, Francis, Virginia, December 30, 1720.—Money Book, 28-34.
Fountaine, Peter, clerk, Virginia, March 30, 1716.—Money Book, 24-371.
Fountaine, James M., Virginia, December 8, 1763.—Money Book, 49-182.
Fowle, John, New England, July 1, 1752.—Money Book, 44-33.
Fraser, —, clerk, Virginia, September 18, 1700.—Money Book, 15-175.
Fraser, George, Virginia, August 20, 1738.—Order Book, 16-338.
Fraser, John, East Florida, April 1, 1769.—Money Book, 51-249.
Fraser, George, Pennsylvania, February 6, 1732-1733.—Money Book, 36-480.
Frazer, Patrick, Bahama Islands, August 30, 1792.—Money Book, 60-91.
Frazier, William, New Jersey, January 12, 1766 (?).—Money Book, 50-233.
Freeman, Arthur, Antigua, June 21, 1785.—Money Book, 57-35.
Frinh (Finch?), Samuel, Georgia, December 8, 1763.—Money Book, 49-182.
Fullerton, David, Dominica, June 23, 1767.—Money Book, 50-234.
Fulton, Mr. John, M.A., South Carolina, April 4, 1730.—Treasury Board Papers, vol. 273-41. Warrant dated April 15, 1730.—Money Book, 35-89.
Fultum, Thomas, clerk, Jamaica, January 21, 1719-1720.—Money Book, 28-34. Son of Robert Fultum, of Guanabo, Jamaica, clerk. Matriculated 1715 (Foster).

Fulwood, Samuel, clerk, Barbadoes, June 18, 1701.—Money Book, 15-185.
Fyfe, William, Virginia, September 24, 1729.—Money Book, 34-509.

Gaillard, Edward, Montserrat, June 1, 1742.—Money Book, 41-4. Order Book, 17-318. Gaillardy, Edward, son of Lewis Gaillard, of Hampstead, Middlesex. B.A. 1738-1739.
Galpine, Calvin, Jamaica, April 29, 1721.—Money Book, 28-34. Son of Calvin, of Taunton, Somerset. Matriculated 1720 (Foster).
Gantt, Edward, Maryland, February 20, 1770.—Money Book, 51-249.
Garden, James, Virginia, September 25, 1754.—Money Book, 45-111.
Garden, Alexander, South Carolina, April 28, 1743.—Money Book, 41-4. Nephew to Commissary Garden, who was born in Scotland, 1685. Died 1783 (Sprague).
Gardner, Robert, Virginia, September 23, 1735.—Money Book, 38-33.
Garrow, David, South Carolina, August 28, 1745.—Money Book, 42-52.
Garzia, John, Virginia, notwithstanding like sum has been paid before for his passage to the Bahama Islands, but that he met with an unexpected obstruction at Cork, April 8, 1724.—Money Book, 31-51.
Garzia, John, Bahama Islands, August 9, 1723.—Money Book, 30-168.
Gavin, Anthony, Virginia, June 17, 1735.—Money Book, 38-33.
Gawkin, Thomas, Virginia, January 12, 1770.—Money Book, 51-249.
Geessendanner, John, South Carolina, October 3, 1749.—Money Book, 43-73.
Gellibrand, —, New York, 29 May, 1690.—Treasury Papers, vol. 8-38.
Gemurill, John, Virginia, September 24, 1729.—Money Book, 34-507.
Gibbs, William, New England, October 11, 1744.—Money Book, 41-420.
Giberne, Isaac William, Virginia, February 12, 1765.—Money Book, 49-306.
Giffard, John, schoolmaster, Leeward Islands, August 27, 1703. Money Book, 16-422.
Gifford, Jonathan, Yale, Montserrat, March 1, 1710-1711.—Money Book, 21-32.

Gigwillatt, James, clerk, America, November 15, 1709.—Money Book, 20-179.
Giles, Samuel, Pennsylvania, January 2, 1766.—Money Book, 50-2. Son of James Giles, of City of Bristol. B.A. 1746 (Foster).
Gilmore, Joseph Dent, Grenada, November 10, 1801.—Money Book, 63-15.
Glasgow, John, Antegoa, March 10, 1707-1708.—Money Book, 19-200.
Glen, William, clerk, Maryland, January 21, 1707-1708.—Money Book, 19-166.
Goldie, George, Virginia, March 3, 1766.—Money Book, 50-2.
Gordon, William, clerk, North Carolina, September 26, 1707.—Money Book, 19-87.
Gordon, —, clerk, New York, August 11 (?), 1702.—Money Book, 16-68. Tre. papers give Patrick, vol. 80-94.
Gordon, William, clerk, Barbadoes, May 31, 1699.—Money Book, 14-369.
Gordon, William, Island of Ex, June 8, 1789.—Money Book, 59-246.
Gordon, William, West Florida, August 13, 1767.—Money Book, 50-234.
Gordon, William, Virginia, June 16, 1775.—Money Book, 53-172.
Gourdon, John, clerk, Maryland, schoolmaster, December 27, 1695.—Money Book, 13-51.
Gourdon, William, clerk, Barbadoes, January 10, 1700-1701.—Money Book, 15-233.
Gowndrel, Rev. Mr. George, appointed a priest in Maryland, March 31, 1770.—Exchequer of Receipt, vol. 407.
Gowndvill, George, Maryland, April 3, 1770.—Money Book, 51-249.
Gowie, Robert, South Carolina, October 23, 1733.—Money Book, 37-37.
Grace, Isaac, clerk, Antegoa, December 4, 1710.—Money Book, 20-440.
Grace, Isaac, Jamaica, February 25, 1705-1706.—Money Book, 18-165.
Grace, Isaac, Virginia, August 5, 1703.—Money Book, 16-410.
Graham, Mr., Maryland, March 12, 1773.—Money Book, 52-41.
Grant, Alexander, Antegoa, January 10, 1748-1749.—Money Book, 43-73.
Graves, Matthew, New England, October 28, 1747.—Money Book, 42-52.
Graves, John, New England, May 18, 1755.—Money Book, 45-111.

Emigrant Ministers to America 31

Gray, Samuel, clerk, Antegoa, December 4, 1710.—Money Book, 20-440.
Gray, Samuel, clerk, Maryland, October 16, 1705.—Money Book, 18-43.
Grayson, Spence, Virginia, June 26, 1771. — Money Book, 52-40.
Green, Joseph, South Carolina, March 24, 1762.—Money Book, 48-155.
Green, George, St. Vincent, March 31, 1778.—Money Book, 54-106.
Gregg, James, clerk, St. Christopher's, March 13, 1710-1711. Money Book, 21-41.
Griffith, David, New Jersey, September 3, 1770.—Money Book, 51-249. Born New York, 1742; died August 3, 1789 (Sprague).
Griffith, David, clerk, Leeward Islands, June 28, 1714.— Money Book, 23-156.
Griffith, Ro., clerk, Pennsylvania, May 5, 1710.—Money Book, 20-274.
Griffiths, Samuel, clerk, South Christopher's, March 6, 1715-1716.—Money Book, 24-386.
Groombridge, Henry, Bahamas, February 12, 1802.—Money Book, 63-15.
Gueny, Lewis, Quebec, April 25, 1775.—Money Book, 53-172.
Gunning, Francis, Jamaica, July 27, 1720.—Money Book, 28-34.
Gurey, George, Virginia, October 4, 1764. — Money Book, 49-306.
Guthire, William, clerk, Jamaica, December 20, 1709.—Money Book, 20-196.
Guy, William, South Carolina, schoolmaster, January 23, 1711-1712.—Money Book, 21-419.
Guy, William, clerk, New York, June 26, 1705.—Money Book, 17-393.

Hackett, Walter, Pennsylvania, March 4, 1728-1729.—Money Book, 34-340.
Haddock, Cookson, Island of Norfolk, December 13, 1798.— Money Book, 62-188.
Hager, Frederick, clerk, minister to the Palatines at New York, January 5, 1709-1710.—Money Book, 20-208.
Haliday, Thomas, East Jersey, October 10, 1710.—Money Book, 20-397.
Hall, Clement, appointed a minister to four northern counties of North Carolina, January 14, 1744.—Money Book, 41-4.
Hall, Thomas, Virginia, May 20, 1774.—Money Book, 52-41.

Hall, Henry, Maryland, January 11, 1697-1698.—Money Book, 13-424.
Halyburton, William, Virginia, September 5, 1766.—Money Book, 50-2.
Hamilton, William Vaughan, Nevis, June 22, 1805.—Money Book, 63-15.
Hamilton, —, clerk, Leeward Islands, schoolmaster, March 24, 1700-1701.—Money Book, 15-259.
Hamilton, Bell, Maryland, October 27, 1747.—Money Book, 42-52.
Hanna, William, Virginia, June 18, 1772.—Money Book, 52-40.
Harlaw, Andrew, Virginia, January 29, 1721-1722.—Money Book, 29-203.
Harman, Samuel Wickham, Antigua, June 23, 1794.—Money Book, 61-42.
Harris, Thomas, Barbadoes, February 9, 1757.—Money Book, 46-62.
Harris, Henry, clerk, returns to Boston, in New England. Has been over to solicit some new establishment for the ministers in that country, April 30, 1715.—Money Book, 23-555.
Harris, John, Newfoundland, June 6, 1788.—Money Book, 59-246.
Harris, Henry, clerk, New England, February 21, 1707-1708.—Money Book, 19-182.
Harris, Robert, Jamaica, March 13, 1754.—Money Book, 45-111. Son of Stephen, of Chrestledon, Cheshire. B.A. 1751.
Harris, Richard, Barbadoes, January 16, 1760.—Money Book, 47-108.
Harrison, Thomas, Maryland, November 16, 1774.—Money Book, 53-172.
Harrison, Thomas, Barbadoes, October 14, 1793.—Money Book, 60-91.
Harrison, Walter Hanson, Maryland, November 16, 1774.—Money Book, 53-172.
Harrison, James, South Carolina, July 1, 1752.—Money Book, 44-33. Son of Leonard of Bongate, Westmoreland. B.A. 1748.
Hart, Samuel, West Florida, May 10, 1764.—Money Book, 49-182.
Harward, Thomas, lecturer, New England, August 12, 1730.—Money Book, 35-89.
Hassill, Thomas, Carolina, schoolmaster, February 13, 1705. Money Book, 18-152.

Emigrant Ministers to America 33

Hawson, William, North Carolina, September 23, 1756.—Money Book, 45-111.
Hays, —, clerk, schoolmaster to the Leeward Islands, October 11, 1700. Money Book, 15-185.
Hebson, Joseph, Barbadoes, October 11, 1768.—Money Book, 51-79.
Henderson, Jacob, Virginia, July 1, 1710.—Money Book, 20-307. Native of Ireland; died January 19, 1735 (Sprague).
Henderson, Jacob, return to Newcastle in Pennsylvania, July 24, 1712.—Money Book, 22-5.
Henley, Samuel, Virginia, January 8, 1770.—Money Book, 51-249.
Henry, Patrick, Virginia, July 31, 1732. Treasury Board Papers, vol. 279-28, September 7, 1732.—Money Book, 36-371.
Herdman, James, Virginia, September 27, 1770.—Money Book, 51-249.
Hesketh, Thomas, Maryland, August 19, 1725.—Money Book, 32-111. Son of Thomas Hesketh, of Croston, Lancashire. Matriculated 1715 (Foster).
Heskith, Thomas, Leeward Islands, November 11, 1698.—Money Book, 14-216.
Hewitt, Richard, North Carolina, December 17, 1724.—Money Book, 31-341.
Heyborne, John Chester, South Carolina, August 15, 1753.—Money Book, 44-33. Son of Richard Heyborne, of St. Giles, Cripplegate, London. Matriculated 1745; D.D. 1763 (Foster).
Hibbert, Thomas, Leeward Islands, June 14, 1733.—Money Book, 37-61.
Hinde, John, South Carolina, February 8, 1771.—Money Book, 51-249.
Hindman, Jacob Henderson, Maryland, March 24, 1770.—Money Book, 51-249.
Hindman, James, clerk, Maryland, January 21, 1707-1708.—Money Book, 19-166.
Hinkesman, John, Plantations, February 10, 1736-1737.—Money Book, 34-249.
Hockley, John, South Carolina, September 13, 1765.—Money Book, 49-306. Son of John Hockley, of Southampton Town. M.A. 1761 (Foster).
Hodges, —, clerk, Jerzies, March 29, 1705.—Money Book, 17-344.
Hodges, Nathaniel, Bahamas, Treasury Minute Book, 29-102-103, August 19, 1742.—Money Book, 41-4.

Holbrook, John, New Jersey, December 13, 1723.—Money Book, 30-168.
Holiday, James, Bermuda, July 23, 1745.—Money Book, 42-52.
Holland, Samuel, Maryland, May 23, 1765.—Money Book, 49-306.
Holland, Thomas, clerk, Bermudas, November 16, 1702.—Money Book, 16-284.
Holme, George, M.A., Leeward Islands, May 29, 1730. Vol. 273-64 Treasury Board Papers. Warrant dated June 2, 1730.—Money Book, 35-89. Son of George Holme, of Penrith. M.A. Camb. 1728 (Foster).
Holmes, John, Georgia, August 12, 1773.—Money Book, 52-41.
Holt, John White, Virginia, June 21, 1776.—Money Book, 53-172.
Holt, Ludlow, Bermuday, March 8, 1777.—Money Book, 53-172.
Holt, Joseph, clerk, Berbados, March 11, 1712-1713.—Money Book, 22-174.
Holt, William, Virginia, June 18, 1772.—Money Book, 52-40.
Honyman, James, formerly chaplain at New York, and is now going chaplain to Road Island, July 12, 1708.—Money Book, 19-300.
Honyman, —, clerk, New York, March 22, 1702-1703.—Money Book, 16-284.
Hooper, William, New England, July 7, 1747.—Money Book, 42-52. Native of Scotland. Died April 14, 1767 (Sprague).
Hopkinson, Thomas, Pennsylvania, October 13, 1773.—Money Book, 52-41.
Horrocks, Rev. James, clerk, Virginia, November 5, 1761.—Exchequer of Receipt, vol. 407.
Horrocks, James, Virginia, November 12, 1761.—Money Book, 48-155.
Horwood, Nathaniel, New York, August 30, 1726.—Money Book, 32-145.
Hotchkis, Richard, Maryland, December 30, 1720.—Money Book, 28-34.
Houseal, Bernard Michael, Halifax, Nova Scotia, January 17, 1786.—Money Book, 58-53.
Houston, James, Maryland, November 17, 1747.—Money Book, 42-52.
Howie, Rev. Alexander, Pennsylvania, February 11, 1730-1731.—Treasury Board Papers, vol. 275-16. Warrant dated February 23, 1730-1731.
Howlett, John, Antegoa, March 15, 1705-1706.—Money Book, 18-171.

Hoyland, Francis, South Carolina, April 1, 1769.—Money Book, 51-249.
Hoyland, Francis, Christophers, January 16, 1754.—Money Book, 45-111.
Hubard, William, Virginia, May 1, 1766.—Money Book, 50-2.
Hubbard, Bela, New England, March 10, 1764.—Money Book, 49-182. Born August 27, 1739, at Guilford, Connecticut. Son of Daniel and Diana Hubbard. Died December 6, 1812 (Sprague).
Hudson, George, clerk, Virginia, July 25, 1694.—Money Book, 12-273.
Hudson, Edward, clerk, Virginia, June 25, 1709.—Money Book, 20-44.
Hughes, Hugh, New York, August 11, 1732.—Treasury Board Papers, vol. 279-42, September 7, 1732. Money Book, 36-371.
Hughes, Thomas, clerk, Virginia, January 31, 1715-1716.—Money Book, 24-363.
Humphreys, Philip, Jamaica, July 4, 1803.—Money Book, 63-15. Son of John Humphreys, of Tewkesbury, co. Gloucester. Matriculated 1784; died January 16, 1834 (Foster).
Humphreys, John, schoolmaster, Philadelphia, November 3, 1710.—Money Book, 20-419.
Humphrys, William, Antigua, October 19, 1780.—Money Book, 55-115.
Hunt, John, Virginia, January 18, 1775.—Money Book, 53-172.
Hunt, John, Bahama Islands, November 9, 1769.—Money Book, 51-249.
Hunt, Isaac, Barbadoes, February 14, 1755.—Money Book, 45-111.
Hunt, Isaac, Trinity Bay, Newfoundland, March 11, 1777.—Money Book, 53-172.
Hunt, Bryan, clerk, Barbadoes, March 16, 1709-1710.—Money Book, 20-236.
Hunt, Brian, Virginia, May 8, 1722.—Money Book, 29-203.
Hunter, Samuel, Maryland, July 19, 1744.—Money Book, 41-4.
Hunter, Henry, Maryland, October 10, 1738.—Money Book, 39-17.
Hurt, John, Virginia, January 18, 1775.—Money Book, 53-172.
Husband, Henry, Antegoa, December 7, 1727.—Money Book, 33-334.
Husbands, Evans Henry, Barbadoes, March 18, 1781.—Money Book, 55-115.

Husbands, John Stewart, Georgia, April 1, 1781.—Money Book, 55-115.
Hutchins, Joseph, Barbadoes, June 18, 1771.—Money Book, 52-40.

Illing, Trangott Frederick, Pennsylvania, September 11, 1772.—Money Book, 52-40.
Inglis, Charles, Pennsylvania, January 10, 1759.—Money Book, 46-62. Son of Archibald Inglis, of Glenkilcan, Ireland; born about 1733. M.A. 1770 (Sprague).
Inman, Abraham, South Carolina, January 31, 1760.—Money Book, 47-108.
Irwyn, George, Maryland, August 24, 1716.—Money Book, 24-473.

Jackson, —, clerk, Newfoundland, March 24, 1700-1701.—Money Book, 15-259.
Jackson, John, Maryland, schoolmaster, March 19, 1725-1726.—Money Book, 32-145.
Jackson, James, Maryland, March 19, 1725-1726.—Money Book, 32-145.
Jacob, Ductie, Pennsylvania, September 24, 1762.—Money Book, 48-272.
Jameson, Walter, Virginia, July 11, 1764.—Money Book, 49-306.
Jameson, John, clerk, Virginia, February 10, 1709-1710.—Money Book, 20-224.
Janatt, Devereux, Virginia, January 26, 1763.—Money Book, 48-272. Jarratt. Born New Kent, Virginia, January 6, 1732-1733. Son of Robert and Sarah Janatt (Sprague).
Jarkman, Robert, Barbadoes, December 28, 1777.—Money Book, 54-106.
Jarratt. See Janatt.
Jarvis, Abraham, New England, March 10, 1764.—Money Book, 49-182. Born Norwalk, Connecticut, May 5, 1739; died May 3, 1813. Son of Samuel Jarvis (Sprague).
Jeafferson, Samuel, Barbadoes, January 12, 1784.—Money Book, 56-249.
Jeffries, Thomas, Maryland, January 11, 1697-1698.—Money Book, 13-424.
Jenkins, Edward, South Carolina, September 11, 1772.—Money Book, 52-40. Son of Edward Jenkins, of Cowbridge, Glamorganshire. B.A. 1767 (Foster).
Jenkins, H., Caicas in Bahamas, November 2, 1796.—Money Book, 61-42.

Emigrant Ministers to America 37

Jenkins, Thomas, clerk, New Jersey, January 27, 1706-1707.—Money Book, 18-391.
Jenmer, Rev. Abraham, clerk, South Carolina, January 28, 1760.—Exchequer of Receipt, vol. 407.
Jenner, George Charles, Harbor Grace, May 26, 1794.—Money Book, 61-42.
Jenney, Robert, schoolmaster, Pennsylvania, June 27, 1714.—Money Book, 23-159.
Jennings, William, Leeward Islands, March 4, 1703-1704.—Money Book, 17-69.
John, Symes, Leeward Islands, October 9, 1767.—Money Book, 50-234.
Johnson, —, senior, chaplain and schoolmaster, Carolina, March 31, 1715.—Money Book, 23-517.
Johnson, William, clerk, Jamaica, February 21, 1703-1704.—Money Book, 17-69.
Johnson, William, Berbadoes, December 3, 1728.—Money Book, 34-189.
Johnson, Thomas, schoolmaster, Jamaica, March 17, 1703-1704.—Money Book, 17-96.
Johnson, Josiah, Virginia, July 22, 1766.—Money Book, 50-234.
Johnson, William, New York, April 14, 1756.—Money Book, 45-111.
Johnson, Samuel, New England, June 28, 1723.—Money Book, 30-78. Born at Guilford, Connecticut, October 14, 1696. Son of Samuel Johnson (Sprague). D.D. 1743-1744 (Foster).
Johnston, Gideon, clerk, Carolina. Another grant, February 11, 1707-1708.—Money Book, 19-172.
Johnston, Francis, North Carolina, October 18, 1768.—Money Book, 51-79.
Johnston, Thomas, Jamaica, April 23, 1803.—Money Book, 63-15.
Johnston, Gideon, clerk. Passage to South Carolina, whither he is returning, having been here some time for the recovery of his health, April 30, 1714.—Money Book, 23-90.
Johnston, Gideon, clerk, Carolina, July 18, 1707.—Money Book, 19-35.
Johnston, Thomas, Maryland, June 25, 1751.—Money Book, 44-33.
Johnston, Andrew, clerk, Jamaica, schoolmaster, July 9, 1706.—Money Book, 18-253.
Johnston, Gideon, clerk, Carolina. Another grant of £20 to him, January 28, 1707-1708. Been detained by the long delay of the fleet and has spent the bounty. Has wife and six children to carry over.—Money Book, 19-68.

Jones, Nicholas, Virginia, December 6, 1723.—Money Book, 30-168.
Jones, Lewis, South Carolina, September 30, 1725.—Money Book, 32-145.
Jones, Henry, Newfoundland, March 11, 1724-1725.—Money Book, 31-171.
Jones, Hugh, Maryland, December 27, 1695.—Money Book, 13-51. Died September 8, 1760, aged 91 (Sprague).
Jones, Hugh, Virginia, September 18, 1724.—Money Book, 31-51.
Jones, —, Virginia (?), September 8, 1699.—Money Book, 14-420.
Jones, —, Virginia, June 7, 1700.—Money Book, 15-120.
Jones, —, clerk, Virginia, March 24, 1700-1701.—Money Book, 15-185.
Jones, Owen, Virginia, September 20, 1703.—Money Book, 16-422.
Jones, James, Jamaica, May 30, 1787.—Money Book, 58-441.
Jones, Hugh, Virginia, September 3, 1716.—Money Book, 24-481.
Jones, Gilbert, Carolina, May 11, 1711.— Money Book, 21-81.
Jones, Walter, North Carolina, December 17, 1724.—Money Book, 31-341. Son of Hector Jones, of Llanelly, co. Carnarvon. Matriculated 1717 (Foster).
Jones, Edward, North Carolina, June 6, 1769.—Money Book, 51-249.
Jones, William, South Carolina, February 20, 1770.—Money Book, 51-249.
Jones, Emanuel, Virginia, November 16, 1774.—Money Book, 53-172.
Jones, James, clerk, Jamaica, February 20, 1707-1708.—Money Book, 19-182.
Jordan, John Nesbit, Dominica, January 22, 1790.—Money Book, 59-246.
Judin, Rev. James (Nedin?), Virginia, November 30, 1732.—Money Book, 36-19.
Julius John Will, Georgia, November 21, 1781.—Money Book, 55-115.
Justice, —, clerk, Barbadoes, October 15, 1700.—Money Book, 15-185.

Kay, Jonathan, clerk, Maryland, August 16, 1711.—Money Book, 21-166.
Keith, James, Virginia, March 4, 1728-1729.—Money Book, 34-340.

Emigrant Ministers to America 39

Keith, Alexander, South Carolina, July 3, 1745.—Money Book, 42-52.
Keith, —, clerk, Maryland, April 25, 1701.—Money Book, 15-259. George Keith born at Aberdeen, Scotland, 1638; died about 1715 (Sprague).
Kelly, John, Jamaica, March 10, 1717-1718.—Money Book, 26-172.
Kemp, Hugh, M.A., Island of Jamaica, April 4, 1730.—Treasury Board Papers, vol. 273-41. Warrant dated April 15, 1730. Money Book, 35-89.
Kendall, John, clerk, Bermudas, December 10, 1695.—Money Book, 13-42.
Kennedy, John, East Florida, January 1, 1777.—Money Book, 53-172.
Kenner, Rodham, Virginia, October 10, 1772.—Money Book, 52-40.
Keogh, John, clerk, Leeward Islands, July 9, 1721.—Money Book, 29-65.
Kerneguy, —, clerk, Virginia, October 11, 1700.—Money Book, 15-185.
Kieth, Mareschal, Bermudas, October 16, 1792.—Money Book, 60-91.
Kilpatrick, Robert, Newfoundland, June 25, 1730.—Money Book, 35-89.
King, William, Bermuda, November 25, 1714.—Money Book, 23-418.
King, Robert Francis, Barbadoes, March 5, 1811.—Money Book, 65-276.
King, W. C. to Douglas and Randon in Nova Scotia, March 11, 1797.—Money Book, 61-42.
King, John, Antigua, September 19, 1750.—Money Book, 43-419.
Kippax, Peter, clerk, Virginia, June 27, 1699.—Money Book, 14-390.
Kirkpatrick, Henry Erskine, Leeward Islands, July 28, 1768. Money Book, 51-79.
Kleig, Samuel, Virginia, June 21, 1768.—Money Book, 51-79.
Knible, Mr., Maryland, December 27, 1695.—Money Book, 13-51.
Knox, James, clerk, St. Christopher's, December 17, 1715.—Money Book, 24-193.
Kocherthal, Joshua. To return to New York, whence he lately came with a representation of the condition of the Palatines, January 28, 1709-1710.—Money Book, 20-222.
Kynaston, John, Virginia, August 16, 1770.—Money Book, 51-249.

Laird, Samuel, Carolina, October 23, 1755.—Money Book, 45-111.
Lambert, John, schoolmaster, South Carolina, October 21, 1727.—Money Book, 33-334.
Lamson, Joseph, New York, July 3, 1745.—Money Book, 42-52.
Lander, Rev. Francis, clerk, Maryland, November 24, 1761.—Exchequer of Receipt, vol. 407.
Lander, Francis, Maryland, November 28, 1761.—Money Book, 48-155.
Lang, John, Virginia, June 4, 1725.—Money Book, 32-4.
Langhorn, John, Canada, May 29, 1787.—Money Book, 58-53.
Langhord, William, South Carolina, August 3, 1750.—Money Book, 43-419.
Langley, John, Isle of Nevis in America, April 3, 1729. Treasury Board Papers, vol. 270-55. Warrant dated June 4, 1729.—Money Book, 34-428. Son of Adam Langley, of Camberwell, Surrey. B.A. 1728 (Foster).
La Piere, John, clerk, Carolina, February 23, 1707-1708.—Money Book, 19-183.
Leadbeater, John, East Florida, May 18, 1773.—Money Book, 52-41.
Leaming, Jeremiah, New England, July 13, 1748.—Money Book, 43-73. Born in Middletown, Connecticut, in 1717; died September, 1804 (Sprague).
Leigh, William, Virginia, April 28, 1772.—Money Book, 52-40.
Leigh, Austin, Dominica, February 21, 1771.—Money Book, 52-20.
Le Jan, Francis, Carolina, November 27, 1705.—Money Book, 18-64.
Leland, John, Virginia, April 25, 1775.—Money Book, 53-172.
Lendrum, Thomas, Virginia, April 4, 1765.—Money Book, 49-306.
Lene, Mr., Maryland, December 27, 1695.—Money Book, 13-51.
Leneve, William, Providence Island, May 31, 1722.—Money Book, 29-203.
Leslie, Andrew, South Carolina, August 5, 1729.—Money Book, 34-491.
Leslie, William, Antegoa, November 17, 1718.—Money Book, 27-48.
Lewis, Jenkins, South Carolina, July 19, 1755.—Money Book, 45-111.
Lewis, Roger, Virginia, April 12, 1709.—Money Book, 19-470.
Lewis, Rees, Cariacon, Granada, October 31, 1785.—Money Book, 58-53. Son of David Lewis, of Llanthogsant, Carnarvonshire. B.A. 1770 (Foster).

Emigrant Ministers to America 41

Lewis, John, South Carolina, September 1, 1768.—Money Book, 51-79.
Liland, John, Virginia, April 25, 1775.—Money Book, 53-172.
Lindsay, Benjamin, Newfoundland, April 18, 1751.—Money Book, 44-33.
Littleton, Thomas, Bermudas, March 31, 1767.—Money Book, 50-234.
Lloyd, Thomas, Nova Scotia, May 19, 1794.—Money Book, 61-42.
Lloyd, Thomas, Bermudas, May 16, 1705.—Money Book, 17-368.
Lloyd, Edward, clerk, Leeward Islands, July 1, 1701.—Money Book, 15-443.
Lloyd, Thomas F., Virginia, May 13, 1766.—Money Book, 50-2.
Load, Thomas, St. Vincent, March 4, 1778.—Money Book, 54-106.
Lock, Richard, Bermudas, July 6, 1743. Treasury Minute Book, 29-289-92.—Money Book, 41-4.
Locke, Rev. Richard, Island of Bermudas, July 4, 1743.—Exchequer of Receipt, vol. 407.
Lockyer, John, clerk, Rhode Island, near New York, October 14, 1701.—Money Book, 15-492.
Lonsdale, William, South Carolina, January 21, 1766.—Money Book, 50-2.
Low, David, Maryland, April 12, 1764.—Money Book, 49-182.
Lucas, Henry, clerk, New England, February 18, 1714-1715.—Money Book, 23-480.
Lucius, Samuel Fred, South Caschna, November 9, 1769.—Money Book, 51-249.
Ludlam, Richard, South Carolina, June 6, 1723.—Money Book, 30-78.
Lunan, Patrick, Virginia, January 29, 1760.—Money Book, 47-108.
Lundie, James, Virginia, January 7, 1766 or 1768.—Money Book, 50-234.
Lynch, W. H., Jamaica, January 20, 1806.—Money Book, 63-15.
Lyon, John, New England, July 11, 1764, Money Book, 49-306.
—Son of Mathew Lyon, of Warrington, Lancashire. Matriculated 1743 (Foster).
Lyons, James, New England, April 28, 1743.—Money Book, 41-4.
Lyth, John, Virginia, December 8, 1763.—Money Book, 49-182.

Macartney, James, North Carolina, September 1, 1768.—Money Book, 51-79.
MacAudlay, John, Jamaica, September 25, 1754.—Money Book, 45-11.
Maccallum, Nevil, Virginia, September 11, 1735.—Money Book, 38-33.
McCalman, Nicholl, clerk, April 29, 1710.—Money Book, 20-271.
McClean, John, Virginia, August 12, 1773.—Money Book, 52-41.
MacClenacan, William, New England, April 4, 1755.—Money Book, 45-111.
McCormick, Robert, Maryland, April 25, 1775.—Money Book, 53-172.
McCrockey, Samuel Smith, December 16, 1772. Money Book, 52-410.
Maccullock, —, Virginia, October 20, 1730.—Money Book, 35-89.
MacDonald, Rev. Daniel, Virginia, October 20, 1731.—Money Book, 36-119.
Macdonald, John, Jamaica, January 30, 1792.—Money Book, 60-91.
M'Dowell, John, North Carolina, August 8, 1753.—Money Book, 44-33.
McFair, John, St. Vincent, November 20, 1798.—Money Book, 62-188.
McGilchrist, William, South Carolina, October 2, 1741.—Money Book, 40-20. Son of James McGilchrist, of Inchianan, Scotland. M.A. 1735 (Foster).
McGill, James, Maryland, April 11, 1728.—Money Book, 33-334.
M'Haen, Robert, New Jersey, May 10, 1757.—Money Book, 46-62.
McHinnon, Daniel, Maryland, January 19, 1769.—Money Book, 51-79.
McIntosh, James, Dominica, January 15, 1771.—Money Book, 50-492.
Mackay, John, Leeward Islands, May 31, 1739.—Money Book, 39-17.
Mackay, William, Virginia, January 8, 1735-1736.—Money Book, 38-33.
McKenly, William, Island of Nevis, March 26, 1773.—Money Book, 52-41.
Mackenzie, William, Virginia, June 11, 1773.—Money Book, 52-41.
Mackenzey, Æneas, New Jersey, May 2, 1705.—Money Book, 17-364.

Mackenzey, Kennith, clerk, Virginia, September 12, 1711.—Money Book, 21-182.
Mackno, Robert, clerk, Maryland, March 27, 1716.—Money Book, 24-386.
Maclamburgh, Samuel, clerk, Maryland, February 26, 1710-1711.—Money Book, 21-25.
McLane, Henry, St. Dominique, July 11, 1764. Money Book, 49-306.
McLaurine, Robert, Virginia, September 5, 1750.—Money Book, 43-419.
McMorran, James, clerk, Maryland, March 16, 1709-1710.—Money Book, 20-237.
McNoe, Robert, Virginia, July 1, 1709.—Money Book, 20-51.
Maconchi, William, Maryland, October 10, 1710.—Money Book, 20-397.
McPherson, John, Maryland, April 18, 1751.—Money Book, 44-33.
Macqueen, —, clerk, Maryland, June 23, 1702.—Money Book, 16-68.
McRae, Christopher, Virginia, January 2, 1766.—Money Book, 50-2.
McRobert, Archibald, Virginia, March 5, 1761.—Money Book, 47-147.
MacSparran, James, New England, November 17, 1720.—Money Book, 28-325. Died December 1, 1757 (Sprague). D.D. 1737 (Foster).
Magaw, Samuel, Pennsylvania, February 24, 1767.—Money Book, 50-234.
Magowan, Walter, Virginia, June 30, 1768.—Money Book, 51-79.
Mainadier, Daniel, clerk, Naraganset, in Connecticut, November 13, 1711.—Money Book, 21-221.
Maitland, John, clerk, Carolina, March 15, 1707-1708.—Money Book, 19-204.
Malcolm, Alexander, Massachusetts Bay, April 3, 1740.—Money Book, 40-20.
Manley, George, clerk, Virginia, November 11, 1715.—Money Book, 24-3.
Mann, Isaac, Dominica, September 12, 1774.—Money Book, 52-41.
Manning, Nathaniel, Virginia, March 20, 1772.—Money Book, 52-40.
Mansfield, Richard, New England, September 14, 1748.—Money Book, 43-73. Born New Haven, Connecticut, in 1724. Son of Jonathan and Susannah Mansfield (Sprague).

Margarett, Francis, Dominica, November 24, 1785.—Money Book, 58-53.
Markby, Thomas, Jamaica, February 21, 1793.—Money Book, 60-91. Son of Thomas Markby, of Marylebone, Middlesex. B.A. 1786 (Foster).
Marshall, Mungo, Virginia, September 20, 1744.—Money Book, 44-4.
Marshall, Thomas, Maryland, January 11, 1697-1698.—Money Book, 13-424.
Marshall, Samuel, Maryland, January 11, 1697-1698.—Money Book, 13-424.
Marshall, William, Barbadoes, December 17, 1800.—Money Book, 62-188.
Marston, Edward, America, April 12, 1715.—Money Book, 23-515.
Marthall, John Rutgers, Connecticut, October 5, 1771.—Money Book, 52-40.
Martel, Jas. Adam de, Nova Scotia, July 8, 1767.—Money Book, 50-234.
Martin, Thomas, Virginia, July 8, 1767.—Money Book, 50-234.
Martin, Nathaniel James, South Carolina, June 11, 1771.—Money Book, 52-40.
Martyn, Charles, South Carolina, September 25, 1751.—Money Book, 44-33. Son of Roger Martyn, of Aylescomb, Devon, clerk. B.A. 1745.
Marye, James, Virginia, December 30, 1755.—Money Book, 45-111.
Masden, —, clerk, Maryland, September 18, 1700.—Money Book, 15-175.
Mashart, Michael, Barbadoes, January 8, 1771.—Money Book, 51-249.
Massett, Francis, Antego, October 11, 1768.—Money Book, 51-79.
Massey, Lee, Virginia, October 21, 1766.—Money Book, 50-234.
Massey, Leigh, Maryland, November 1, 1722.—Money Book, 30-78. Son of James Massey, of Oxmanton, near Dublin. B.A. 1721-1722 (Foster).
Mather, Jos., Maryland, January 8, 1761.—Money Book, 47-108.
Mathews, John, Virginia, July 11, 1764.—Money Book, 49-306.
Mathews, John, St. Vincent's, April 6, 1787.—Money Book, 58-53.
Maule, Robert, North America, February 20, 1706-1707.—Money Book, 18-420.

Emigrant Ministers to America 45

Maury, Mathew, Virginia, September 8, 1769.—Money Book, 51-249.
Maury, James, Virginia, June 29, 1742.—Treasury Minute Book, 29-67, 68.
Maury, William, schoolmaster, North Carolina, May 8, 1723.—Money Book, 30-78.
May, John, Virginia, January 9, 1709-1710.—Money Book, 20-198.
May, William, clerk, Jamaica, October 22, 1719.—Money Book, 27-153.
Maynadier, Daniel, Maryland, January 15, 1761.—Money Book, 47-147.
Mecan, Bernard, clerk, Jamaica, August 12, 1715.—Money Book, 24-6.
Mechlonberg, Mr., Virginia, May 7, 1772.—Money Book, 52-40.
Meldrum, William, Virginia, June 23, 1756.—Money Book, 45-111.
Menzies, Adam, Virginia, January 10, 1750-1751.—Money Book, 43-419.
Merac, John, St. Christopher's, February 16, 1727-1728.—Money Book, 33-334.
Merry, Francis, clerk, South Carolina, July 9, 1721.—Money Book, 29-65.
Messenger, J., Virginia, May 19, 1772.—Money Book, 52-40.
Micklejohn, George, North Carolina, March 29, 1766.—Money Book, 50-2.
Miles, Samuel, clerk, Newfoundland, February 28, 1695-1696.—Money Book, 13-85.
Millechamp, Timothy, South Carolina.—Money Book, 36-119, June 6, 1732. Son of Richard Millechamp, of Abdon, Salop. B.A. 1718 (Foster).
Miller, Benjamin, schoolmaster, Maryland, January 21, 1711-1712.—Money Book, 21-419.
Miller, Joseph, Dominica, October 13, 1773.—Money Book, 52-41.
Miller, William, North Carolina, April 4, 1755.—Money Book, 45-111.
Miller, John, New York, April 27, 1692.—King's Warrant Book, 9-222.
Miller, Ebenezer, New England, October 21, 1727.—Money Book, 33-334. D.D. 1747 (Foster).
Mills, James, Barbadoes, May 8, 1722.—Money Book, 29-203.
Miln, John, New York, September 26, 1727.—Money Book, 33-334.
Milne, Francis, clerk, Maryland, October 27, 1707.—Money Book, 19-102.

Milner, John, New York, March 5, 1761.—Money Book, 47-147.
Mitchell, George, Maryland, October 26, 1774.—Money Book, 52-41.
Mitton, Roger, Virginia, April 27, 1692.—King's Warrant Book, 9-222.
Moe, Irenos, Barbadoes, May 9, 1808.—Money Book, 64-386. Irenæus, son of Cheesman Moe, of Barbadoes. B.A. 1807 (Foster).
Moir, James, North Carolina, November 13, 1739.—Money Book, 17-20.
Monereiff, Robert, Antigua, March 7, 1748-1749.—Money Book, 43-73.
Montgomery, John, Maryland, August 16, 1770.—Money Book, 51-249.
Moore, Rev. W. H. To examine in the Bahamas, August 2, 1796.—Money Book, 61-42. Son of Samuel Moore, of St. Stephen's, Exeter, gent. B.A. 1790 (Foster).
Moore, Lambert, Georgia, November 9, 1781.—Money Book, 55-115.
Moore, Thorrowgood, clerk, America, February 19, 1703-1704.—Money Book, 17-94.
Moore, Benjamin, New York, July 6, 1774.—Money Book, 52-41. Born October 5, 1748, at Newtown, Long Island. Son of Samuel and Sarah (Fish) Moore. Died February 27, 1816 (Sprague).
Moore, J., Bermuda, September 14, 1743.—Money Book, 41-4.
More, —, chaplain going abroad, November 29, 1743.—Treasury Minute Book, 29-357-8.
Moreau, Charles F., South Carolina, February 16, 1773.—Money Book, 52-41.
Morgan, Thomas, South Carolina, June 6, 1769.—Money Book, 51-249.
Morgan, William, Jamaica, September 25, 1773.—Money Book, 52-41.
Morison, Kenneth, Barbadoes, October 24, 1745.—Money Book, 42-52.
Morris, Theophilus, Connecticut, June 4, 1740.—Money Book, 40-20.
Morrison, James, Virginia, May 1, 1776.—Money Book, 53-172.
Morrison, John, Virginia (?), September 8, 1699.—Money Book, 14-420.
Morritt, Thomas, schoolmaster, South Carolina, January 18, 1722-1723.—Money Book, 30-78.
Morthland, David, Maryland, September 1, 1733.—Money Book, 37-37.

Morton, Andrew, New Jersey, March 18, 1760.—Money Book, 47-108.
Moss, Richard, Bahama, February 19, 1767.—Money Book, 50-234.
Mossom, David, clerk, Virginia, August 18, 1718.—Money Book, 27-3.
Mott, —, clerk, New York, February 10, 1701-1702.—Money Book, 16-13.
Munn, Richard, Jamaica, October 16, 1795.—Money Book, 61-42.
Munro, Harry, New York, February 20, 1765.—Money Book, 49-306.
Murray, Alexander, Pennsylvania, June 16, 1762.—Money Book, 48-272.
Musgrave, Dawson, Virginia, February 4, 1747.—Money Book, 42-52.

Nairn, William, Bermuda, May 8, 1722.—Money Book, 29-203.
Nankivel, Rev. Mr., St. Christopher's, December 5, 1796.—Money Book, 61-42.
Napleton, Thomas, Barbadoes, August 6, 1717.—Money Book, 25-320.
Nash, William, Barbadoes, December 17, 1800.—Money Book, 62-188.
Neblett, James Fowler, Barbadoes, June 2, 1796.—Money Book, 61-42.
Nedin (Judin?), Rev. James, Virginia, November 30, 1732.—Money Book, 36-119.
Neill, Hugh, Pennsylvania, May 2, 1750.—Money Book, 43-73.
Nevison, John, Virginia, March 5, 1752.—Money Book, 44-33.
Newberry, John, Leeward Islands, January 19, 1729-1730.—Money Book, 35-89. Son of Henry Newbeny, of Stoke, Surrey. B.A. 1725 (Foster).
Newman, Thomas, North Carolina, October 19, 1701.—Money Book, 29-203.
Newton, Christopher, New England, July 30, 1755.—Money Book, 45-111.
Nicholl, —, clerk, counties next Pennsylvania, May 5, 1703.—Money Book, 16-333.
Nichols, James, Connecticut, February 10, 1774.—Money Book, 52-41.
Nickolles, Robert Bowcher, Barbadoes, April 14, 1768.—Money Book, 50-492. Robert Boucher Nicholls, son of Isaac Nicholls, of Barbadoes, gent. B.A. 1766 (Foster).

Niles, William, Island of Tortola, January 12, 1790.—Money Book, 59-246.
Nobbs, Benjamin, Maryland, January 11, 1697-1698.—Money Book, 13-424.
Norris, William, Georgia, August 20, 1738.—Money Book, 39-17.
Nowell, Thomas, clerk, Leeward Islands, March 27, 1705.—Money Book, 17-344.
Nush, William, Euma in Bahamas, January 18, 1799.—Money Book, 62-188.

Oatoll, Jonathan, New Jersey, January 23, 1767.—Money Book, 50-234.
Obrien, Christopher, clerk, Virginia, April 28, 1707.—Money Book, 18-457.
Ogden, Usal, New Jersey, September 25, 1773.—Money Book, 52-41.
Ogelvie, Walter, Jamaica, March 16, 1709-1710.—Money Book, 19-462.
Ogilvie, James, Virginia, October 5, 1771.—Money Book, 52-40.
Ogilvie, John, New York, July 12, 1749.—Money Book, 43-73. Born at New York in 1722; died November 26, 1774 (Sprague).
Ogle, Henry, clerk, West Indies (?), December 7, 1704.—Money Book, 17-287.
O'Hara, Joseph, Providence in New England, June 4, 1728.—Money Book, 34-27.
Orem, James, New England, October 19, 1721.—Money Book, 29-203.
Orr, Samuel, Leeward Islands, October 10, 1710.—Money Book, 20-397.
Orr, William, South Carolina, October 7, 1736.—Money Book, 38-267.
Orton, Christopher, Georgia, October 2, 1741.—Money Book, 40-20.
Osborne, Nathaniel, clerk, South Carolina, September 24, 1712.—Money Book, 22-61.
Osmond, David, Nova Scotia, February 4, 1793.—Money Book, 60-91.
Outlaw, Samuel, Leeward Islands, May 13, 1705.—Money Book, 17-373.
Owen, Robert, clerk. Was called home from Maryland upon hopes of an estate, but being disappointed, he is desirous to return to Maryland. September 13, 1705.—Money Book, 18-20.

Emigrant Ministers to America 49

Owen, Gronow, Jamaica, November 3, 1757.—Money Book, 46-62. Son of Owen Owen, of Llanfair, Mathafarn. Matriculated 1742 (Foster).
Owen, —, Maryland, July 28, 1698.—Money Book, 14-171.
Owen, —, Maryland, August 31, 1699.—Money Book, 14-420.

Page, Bernard, Pennsylvania, September 11, 1772.—Money Book, 52-40.
Pasmer, Henry, Maryland, January 11, 1697-1698.—Money Book, 13-424.
Pasteur, James, Virginia, January 16, 1754.—Money Book, 45-111.
Pasteur, Charles, Virginia, March 19, 1735-1736.—Money Book, 38-267.
Patten, Thomas, clerk, Virginia, May 5, 1710.—Money Book, 20-274.
Patterson, John, Maryland, June 14, 1768.—Money Book, 51-79.
Paxton, Robert, clerk, Virginia, October 20, 1709.—Money Book, 20-169-175.
Payne, William Maynard, Barbadoes, May 21, 1802.—Money Book, 63-15.
Pearce, Offspring, South Carolina, October 8, 1761.—Money Book, 48-155.
Pearson, —, schoolmaster, Maryland, October 10, 1710.—Money Book, 20-397.
Peart, Francis, Virginia, November 19, 1730.—Money Book, 35-89. Son of Francis Peart, of St. John's, city of Worcester. Matriculated 1719 (Foster).
Peasley, William, Newfoundland, March 8, 1742-1743.—Money Book, 41-4.
Peat, Joshua, Jamaica, November 13, 1733 (wrongly dated November 13, 1732).—Money Book, 37-37.
Peat, Joshua, Jamaica, October 8, 1746.—Money Book, 42-52.
Peirce, James, South Carolina, October 12, 1769.—Money Book, 51-249.
Peirson, John, New Jersey, September 1, 1733.—Money Book, 37-37.
Pemberton, Robert, Nevisin, January 17, 1786.—Money Book, 58-53. Son of Robert Pemberton, of Isle of Nevis, arm. Matriculated 1767 (Foster).
Pender, Edzard, Virginia, July 12, 1726.—Money Book, 32-145.
Penny, John, Jamaica, December 1, 1761.—Money Book, 48-155.

Perkins, Jonathan, Barbadoes, December 1, 1737.—Money Book, 39-17.
Pettigrew, Charles, North Carolina, March 7, 1775.—Money Book, 53-172. Son of James Pettigrew; died 1807 (Sprague).
Phillips, William, Virginia, January 8, 1735-1736.—Money Book, 38-33.
Phillips, John, Jamaica, March 19, 1725-1726.—Money Book, 32-145.
Phillips, Francis, clerk, Maryland, December 10, 1711.—Money Book, 21-260.
Phillips, Thomas, clerk, Virginia, August 9, 1715.—Money Book, 24-4.
Phillips, John Lott, North Carolina, June 21, 1776.—Money Book, 53-172.
Phillips, Thomas, clerk, Antegoa, May 21, 1707.—Money Book, 18-465.
Picart, Samuel, clerk, Leeward Islands, February 19, 1708-1709.—Money Book, 19-450.
Piggot, George, Connecticut, January 9, 1721-1722.—Money Book, 29-203.
Pilgrim, John Frere, Barbadoes, November 20, 1798.—Money Book, 62-188.
Pillin, Thomas, Rhode Island, February 20, 1754.—Money Book, 45-111.
Pinder, William Lake, Barbadoes, May 9, 1808.—Money Book, 64-386.
Plant, Mathias, New England, October 19, 1721.—Money Book, 29-203.
Platt, Francis, Maryland, January 11, 1697-1698.—Money Book, 13-424.
Plessis, Peter du, South Carolina, June 3, 1736.—Money Book, 38-267. Son of Franc Plessis, of Shoreditch, London, clerk. Matriculated 1730 (Foster).
Poger, Thomas, clerk, New York, December 28, 1709.—Money Book, 20-202.
Pool, Thomas, Jamaica, August 12, 1773.—Money Book, 52-41. Son of John Pool, of Jamaica, clerk. Matriculated 1767 (Foster).
Porter, Charles, Jamaica, August 12, 1715.—Money Book, 24-6.
Porter, John, Maryland, June 14, 1768.—Money Book, 51-79.
Pouderous, Albert, Carolina, November 9, 1720.—Money Book, 28-325.
Poulteney, Francis, Virginia, January 8, 1735-1736.—Money Book, 38-33.

Emigrant Ministers to America 51

Pow, William, North Carolina, January 31, 1748-1749.—Money Book, 43-73.
Powell, Thomas, Nevis, October 4, 1739.—Money Book, 40-20.
Pownall, Benjamin, clerk, Virginia, July 4, 1715.—Money Book, 24-62.
Preade, Robert, Virginia, April 12, 1758.—Money Book, 46-62.
Price, Jacob, Newfoundland, May 24, 1705.—Money Book, 17-364.
Price, Walter, St. John's, Newfoundland, April 17, 1784.—Money Book, 57-69.
Price, Thomas, Virginia, January 23, 1760.—Money Book, 47-108.
Price, Roger, New England, March 18, 1728-1729.—Money Book, 34-340. Son of William Price, Rector of Whitfield, Northampton, England (Sprague).
Prince, John, clerk, Bermudas, July 10, 1717.—Money Book, 25-264.
Pritchyard, Thomas, New York, November 30, 1703.—Money Book, 17-23.
Proctor, William, Virginia, August 21, 1745.—Money Book, 42-52.
Purcell, Robert, South Carolina, April 1, 1769.—Money Book, 51-249. Son of Robert Purcell, of city of Bristol, clerk. Matriculated 1751 (Foster).
Purcell, Henry, South Carolina, April 3, 1770.—Money Book, 51-249. Son of George Purcell, of Hereford. B.A. 1763 (Foster).

Quincy, Samuel, Georgia, April 2, 1733.—Money Book, 36-480.

Raddish, T., Upper Canada, August 2, 1796.—Money Book, 61-42. Son of William Raddish, of London. M.A. 1796.
Rainsford, Giles, Maryland, September 3, 1716.—Money Book, 24-481.
Ramsay, James, Charibbee Islands, November 28, 1761.—Money Book, 48-155.
Ramsay, John, Virginia, September 25, 1751.—Money Book, 44-33.
Ray, James, Leeward Islands, January 23, 1705-1706.—Money Book, 18-64.
Raynsford, clerk, Jamaica, June 15, 1702.—Money Book, 16-68.
Read, Thomas, Maryland, September 25, 1773.—Money Book, 52-41.

Read, Delahay, St. Christopher's, February 12, 1760.—Money Book, 47-108.
Read, John, Virginia, June 13, 1737.—Money Book, 39-17.
Reading, William, Maryland, January 11, 1697-1698.—Money Book, 13-424.
Reading, Philip, Pennsylvania, April 17, 1746.—Money Book, 42-52. Son of William Reading, of St. Alphage, London, clerk. Matriculated 1738 (Foster).
Reid, John, North Carolina, April 4, 1745.—Money Book, 41-4.
Rennie, John, Georgia, December 22, 1773.—Money Book, 52-41.
Renny, Robert, Virginia, July 11, 1764.—Money Book, 49-306.
Reynolds, James, clerk, New York, May 6, 1709.—Money Book, 20-13.
Rhonald, Alexander, Virginia, May 14, 1760.—Money Book, 47-108.
Richards, John, Virginia, August 13, 1724.—Money Book, 31-51.
Richardson, —, Virginia, July 12, 1700.—Money Book, 15-120.
Richtie, David, Dominica, June 3, 1801.—Money Book, 62-188.
Roberson, John, St. Christopher's, June 16, 1775.—Money Book, 53-172.
Roberts, Alexander, Jamaica, October 19, 1780.—Money Book, 55-115.
Roberts, Edward, clerk, New Jersey, December 10, 1705.—Money Book, 18-85.
Robertson, John, Virginia, February 4, 1745-1746.—Money Book, 42-52.
Robertson, Moses, Virginia, March 4, 1728-1729.—Money Book, 34-340.
Robertson, Alexander, Jamaica, March 7, 1775.—Money Book, 53-172.
Robertson, James, Virginia, January 15, 1717-1718.—Money Book, 26-159.
Robertson, Thomas, Hudson Island (?), North America, April 1, 1786.—Money Book, 58-53.
Robertson, Robert, clerk, Leeward Islands, January 21, 1706-1707.—Money Book, 18-375.
Robinson, William, Virginia, September 25, 1746.—Money Book, 42-52. Son of Christopher Robinson, of Virginia. B.A. 1740 (Foster).
Robinson, John, St. Christopher's, June 16, 1775.—Money Book, 53-172.

Roe, Stephen, South Carolina, April 5, 1737.—Money Book, 38-33.
Rogers, Henry, St. Vincent, March 5, 1811.—Money Book, 65-276.
Ronald. See Rhonald.
Rose, Daniel Warner, Long Island, in Bahamas, November 13, 1797.—Money Book, 61-42.
Rose, Patrick, Barbadoes, September 14, 1727.—Money Book, 33-333.
Rose (Ross), Charles, Barbadoes, January 11, 1731-1732.—Money Book, 36-119.
Rose, Charles, Virginia, March 15, 1736-1737.—Money Book, 38-33.
Ross, George, New Jerzey, May 2, 1705.—Money Book, 17-364.
Ross, Anneas, Pennsylvania, February 26, 1740-1741.—Money Book 40-20.
Ross. See Rose.
Rosse, John, Maryland, October 10, 1754.—Money Book, 45-111.
Rowan, John, North Carolina, September 24, 1747.—Money Book, 42-52.
Rowe, Jacob, Virginia, February 14, 1758.—Money Book, 46-62.
Rudd, Thomas, schoolmaster, South Carolina, January 28, 1711-1712.—Money Book, 21-419.
Rudd, —, Virginia, August 31, 1699.—Money Book, 14-420.
Rudd, William, Jamaica, April 15, 1706.—Money Book, 18-191.

Saer, Richard, Barbadoes, March 30, 1757.—Money Book, 46-62.
St. Clare, —, clerk, Pennsylvania, August 31, 1709.—Money Book, 20-126.
St. John, Richard, Bahamas, October 1, 1745.—Money Book, 42-52.
Saunders, John Hyde, Virginia, October 10, 1772.—Money Book, 52-40.
Sayer, James, New York, October 12, 1774.—Money Book, 53-172.
Sayre, John, in and throughout America, October 11, 1768.—Money Book, 51-79.
Schwab, Christopher E., South Carolina, June 11, 1771.—Money Book, 52-40.
Scott, Alexander, Virginia, October 10, 1710.—Money Book, 20-397.

A List of

Scott, Robert, clerk, Maryland, March 10, 1707-1708.—Money Book, 19-200.
Scott, John, Maryland, April 1, 1769.—Money Book, 51-249.
Scott, William, Charibbee Islands, July 11, 1764.—Money Book, 49-306.
Scott, John, clerk, Jamaica, March 6, 1715-1716.—Money Book, 24-386.
Seabury, Samuel, New Jersey, January 16, 1754.—Money Book, 45-111. Born at Groton, Connecticut, November 30, 1729. Son of Rev. Samuel Seabury (Sprague).
Seabury, Samuel, New England, October 20, 1730.—Money Book, 35-89. D.D. 1777 (Foster).
Seagood, George, Virginia, December 12, 1716.—Money Book, 25-145.
Sebastian, Benjamin, Virginia, October 2, 1766.—Money Book, 20-234.
Selden, William, Virginia, March 14, 1771.—Money Book, 52-40.
Selden, Miles, Virginia, January 21, 1752.—Money Book, 44-33.
Seovil, James, New England, April 11, 1759.—Money Book, 46-62.
Serjeant, Wenwood, South Carolina, February 1, 1757.—Money Book, 46-62.
Serling, James, Maryland, April 22, 1752.—Money Book, 44-33.
Seymour, James, South Carolina, September 25, 1771.—Money Book, 52-40.
Shanks, Edward, Jamaica, February 10, 1706-1707.—Money Book, 18-412.
Sharp, —, Virginia, August 31, 1699.—Money Book, 14-420.
Sharp, John, clerk, Leeward Islands, February 27, 1700-1701.—Money Book, 15-259.
Shaw, Robert, Musquito Shore, July 6, 1774.—Money Book, 52-41.
Shaw, George, St. Christopher's, June 22, 1787.—Money Book, 58-441.
Shaw, William, clerk, New England, December 22, 1714.—Money Book, 23-430.
Sheild, Samuel, Virginia, January 18, 1775.—Money Book, 53-172.
Shene, George, South Carolina, December 17, 1761.—Money Book, 48-155.
Shepeard, Richard, clerk, Virginia, February 28, 1706-1707.—Money Book, 18-422.

Shepheard, Rev. Henry, Leeward Islands, June 5, 1739.—Money Book, 39-380.
Shepherd, Mr., Antigua, March 12, 1773.—Money Book, 52-41.
Sherston, John, Antegoa, November 12, 1729.—Money Book, 35-89.
Shervington, William, Antigua, January 16, 1754.—Money Book, 45-111.
Shield, Samuel, Virginia, January 18, 1775.—Money Book, 53-172.
Shorthose, Henry, Virginia, February 27, 1732-1733.—Money Book, 36-480.
Shreve, Thomas, B.A., late of King's College, New York, Parrsboro', Nova Scotia, June 11, 1787.—Money Book, 58-53.
Simmonds, John, Jamaica, September 26, 1787.—Money Book, 58-441.
Simpson, Bolton, Charleston, September 11, 1745.—Money Book, 42-52.
Skaife, John, clerk, Virginia, September 13, 1708.—Money Book, 19-357.
Skelson, William, Antegoa, April 8, 1724.—Money Book, 31-51.
Skinner, William, schoolmaster, Philadelphia, June 10, 1718.—Money Book, 26-159.
Skippson, Samuel, clerk, Maryland, April 6, 1714.—Money Book, 23-63.
Skyring, Henry, Virginia, October 19, 1763.—Money Book, 49-182.
Slade, S., clerk, Leeward Islands, November 21, 1695.—Money Book, 13-39.
Sloan, Samuel, Maryland, January 2, 1766.—Money Book, 50-2.
Small, Robert, South Carolina, June 21, 1738.—Money Book, 39-17.
Smith, William, clerk, Leeward Islands, February 3, 1715-1716.—Money Book, 24-368.
Smith, Joseph, Virginia, September 21, 1727.—Money Book, 33-333.
Smith, Andrew, clerk, Jamaica, May 19, 1705.—Money Book, 17-369.
Smith, John, "voyage to America to make tryall of a rich Silver Mine. £200 for pasage money," June 23, 1698.—King's Warrant Book, 12-515.
Smith, Simon, Jamaica, January 7, 1694.—Money Book, 12-418.

Smith, Robert, South Carolina, October 12, 1769.—Money Book, 51-249. Born at Norfolk, England, August 25, 1732; died October 28, 1801 (Sprague).
Smith, Haddon, Jamaica, January 5, 1767.—Money Book, 20-234.
Smith, Thomas, Virginia, October 11, 1752.—Money Book, 44-33.
Smith, William, Virginia, September 24, 1729.—Money Book, 34-506.
Smith, William, Bahamas, April 6, 1733.—Money Book, 36-480.
Smith, Charles, Virginia, October 28, 1740.—Money Book, 40-20.
Smith, James, clerk, Virginia, January 12, 1702-1703.—Money Book, 16-250.
Smith, Haddon, South Carolina, September 11, 1772.—Money Book, 52-40.
Smith, William, Pennsylvania, January 16, 1754.—Money Book, 45-111. Born at Aberdeen, Scotland, about 1727; died May 14, 1813 (Sprague).
Snow, John, Bahama Islands, July 16, 1746.—Money Book, 42-52.
Somervill, James, Antigua, March 8, 1768.—Money Book, 50-492.
Span, John, Virginia, "to go in place of Bruen, who had £20 to go to Leeward Islands, but now refuses," October 25, 1710.—Money Book, 20-403.
Spence, James, Jamaica, January 29, 1708-1709.—Money Book, 19-434.
Spencer, George, New Jersey, January 23, 1767.—Money Book, 50-234.
Spencer, Archibald, Virginia, September 20, 1749.—Money Book, 43-73.
Squire, Richard, clerk, Virginia, November 30, 1702.—Money Book, 16-202.
Staige, Theodosius, Virginia, June 4, 1725.—Money Book, 32-4.
Standard, Thomas, Virginia, May 7, 1723.—Money Book, 30-78.
Standforth, William, New York, July 22, 1775.—Money Book, 53-172.
Standish, David, South Carolina, August 5, 1724.—Money Book, 31-51.
Stanser, Robert, Halifax in Nova Scotia, June 24, 1791.—Money Book, 60-91. Son of John Stanser, of Wales, Yorks. Matriculated 1751 (Foster); died 1829 (*Gentleman's Magazine*).

Emigrant Ministers to America 57

Stephen, John, Tobago, October 4, 1764.—Money Book, 49-306.
Sterling, James, Maryland, September 16, 1737.—Money Book, 39-17.
Steuart, John, New York, September 3, 1770.—Money Book, 51-249.
Stevenson, James, Virginia, October 11, 1768.—Money Book, 51-79.
Stewart, Alexander, clerk, New York, April 17, 1703.—Money Book, 16-284.
Stewart, Thomas, Jamaica, August 30, 1792.—Money Book, 60-91.
Stewart, Alexander, North Carolina, June 27, 1753.—Money Book, 44-33.
Stith, William, Virginia, April 12, 1731.—Money Book, 35-89. Son of John Stith, of the Virgin Islands. M.A. 1730 (Foster).
Stockhouse, Thomas, South Carolina, December 23, 1704.—Money Book, 17-287.
Stokes, Joseph, South Carolina, October 30, 1711.—Money Book, 48-155. Son of Joseph Stokes, of Bristol. M.A. 1757 (Foster).
Stone, Robert, South Carolina, July 12, 1749.—Money Book, 43-73. Son of Robert Stone, of Taunton Deane. B.A. 1742-1743 (Foster).
Stoope, Peter, New York, February 15, 1723-1724.—Money Book, 31-51.
Strachan, James, clerk, Jamaica, June 24, 1713.—Money Book, 22-257.
Strahan, David, clerk, Virginia, October 18, 1715.—Money Book, 24-158.
Straichan, Adam, schoolmaster, Leeward Islands, November 29, 1700.—Money Book, 15-185.
Stringer, Mr., Philadelphia, March 12, 1773.—Money Book, 52-41.
Stuart, William, Virginia, October 8, 1746.—Money Book, 42-52.
Stuart, James, Virginia, October 2, 1766.—Money Book, 50-234.
Sturgeon, William, Pennsylvania, December 1, 1747.—Money Book, 42-52.
Sturges, Daniel, Virginia, November 28, 1771.—Money Book, 52-40.
Swift, William, Bermuda, May 8, 1722.—Money Book, 29-203.
Swynfen, Henry, Virginia, December 30, 1720.—Money Book, 28-34. Son of John Swynfen, of St. Albans, Wood Street. B.A. 1720 (Foster).

Taaffe, Henry, Jamaica, September 25, 1751.—Money Book, 44-33.
Taylor, Charles Edward, North Carolina, January 8, 1771.—Money Book, 51-249.
Taylor, William, Leeward Islands, January 26, 1770.—Money Book, 51-249.
Taylor, Ebenezer, South Carolina, November 13, 1711.—Money Book, 21-221.
Taylor, Rev. Samuel Okes, St. Christopher's, May 18, 1796.—Money Book, 61-42.
Taylor, Daniel, Virginia, May 30, 1727.—Money Book, 33-318.
Tennant, James, clerk, Virginia, May 28, 1708.—Money Book, 19-254.
Theodore, Esdras, Virginia, July 12, 1726.—Money Book, 32-145.
Thomas, Walter, Antegoa, December 30, 1720.—Money Book, 28-34.
Thomas, William, Barbadoes, January 6, 1791.—Money Book, 60-91.
Thomas, George, clerk, New York, April 1, 1704.—Money Book, 17-106.
Thomas, Samuel, clerk, North Carolina, August 11, 1702.—Money Book, 16-68.
Thomas, —, schoolmaster, Pennsylvania, July 5, 1700.—Money Book, 15-143.
Thomas, John, M.A., Carolina, January 21, 1729-1730.—Treasury Board Papers, vol. 173-9.
Thomas, Edwin, Island of Nevisin, December 22, 1747.—Money Book, 42-52.
Thompson, William, Pennsylvania, January 16, 1760,—Money Book, 47-108.
Thompson, Andrew, clerk, Virginia, July 24, 1712.—Money Book, 22-5.
Thompson, James, clerk, Jamaica, November 7, 1707.—Money Book, 19-112.
Thompson, Ebenezer, New England, September 28, 1743.—Money Book, 41-4.
Thompson, George, Virginia, June 20, 1726.—Money Book, 32-145.
Thompson, William, Leeward Islands, November 12, 1729.—Money Book, 35-89.
Thompson, John, Maryland, November 8, 1739.—Money Book, 40-0.
Thompson, Thomas, New Jersey, July 20, 1748.—Money Book, 43-73.

Emigrant Ministers to America 59

Thompson, Thomas, New Jersey, April 2, 1745.—Money Book, 41-4.
Thomson, —, appointed a minister abroad, September 21, 1743. Treasury Minute Book, 29-327-9.
Thomson, James, Virginia, March 7, 1769.—Money Book, 51-79.
Thomson, Robert, clerk, factory of Petersburgh, April 28, 1713. —Money Book, 22-214.
Thomson, Thomas, clerk, Maryland, March 10, 1710-1711.— Money Book, 21-32.
Thomson, John, Bermudas, October 3, 1801.—Money Book, 63-15.
Thorn, Sydinham, Pennsylvania, September 12, 1774.—Money Book, 52-41.
Thornton, Rev. Thomas, clerk, Maryland, September 22, 1754. —Exchequer of Receipt, vol. 407.
Thornton, Thomas, Maryland, October 10, 1754.—Money Book, 45-111.
Thursby, —, Maryland, July 28, 1698.—Money Book, 14-171.
Thurston, Charles Mynn, Virginia, August 15, 1765.—Money Book, 49-306.
Tibbs, Wm., Maryland, May 7, 1701.—Money Book, 15-408.
Tillard, —, clerk, Virginia, June 15, 1702.—Money Book, 16-68.
Tingley, Mr., New Jersey, March 12, 1773.—Money Book, 52-41.
Tinney, William, clerk, Virginia, October 10, 1709.—Money Book, 20-130.
Tissot, John James, South Carolina, August 5, 1729.—Money Book, 34-491.
Tittle, John, New York, September 24, 1729.—Money Book, 34-506.
Tizard, George, Bahama, January 23, 1767,—Money Book, 50-234.
Toale, William, North Carolina, December 8, 1762.—Money Book, 48-272.
Todd, Christopher, Virginia, May 9, 1775.—Money Book, 53-172.
Todd, Thomas, clerk, Jamaica, March 27, 1704.—Money Book, 17-97.
Todd, Thomas, Jamaica, September 9, 1698.—Money Book, 14-154.
Tonke, Thomas, Jamaica, January 12, 1709-1710.—Money Book, 20-198.
Tookerman, Josiah, clerk, Jamaica, schoolmaster, October 22, 1709.—Money Book, 20-198.

Tookerman, Josias, clerk, Leeward Islands, November 6, 1705.—Money Book, 18-61.
Topp, Edward, Maryland, January 11, 1697-1698.—Money Book, 13-424.
Tosh, —, schoolmaster at Jamaica, January 5, 1699-1700.—Money Book, 15-42.
Townsend Epenatus, New York, January 7, 1768.—Money Book, 50-234.
Tracy, Alexander, schoolmaster, South Carolina, July 1, 1715.—Money Book, 24-45.
Tracy, Alexander, schoolmaster, Philadelphia, March 20, 1710-1711.—Money Book, 21-45.
Treadwell, Agus, New Jersey, May 7, 1762.—Money Book, 48-272.
Trendall, Henry, Maryland, March 31, 1767.—Money Book, 50-234.
Tresham, Richard, clerk, Jamaica, March 19, 1717-1718.—Money Book, 26-172.
Troller, John, Tobago, January 10, 1769.—Money Book, 51-79.
Trotter, George, Maryland, January 11, 1697-1698.—Money Book, 13-424.
Troutbeck, John, Massachusetts Bay, May 15, 1754.—Money Book, 45-111. Son of George Troutbeck, of Blencow, Cumberland, B.A. 1741 (Foster).
Tuazier, William, New Jersey, January 12, 1766.—Money Book, 50-233.
Tucker, Thomas, Jamaica, June 6, 1707.—Money Book, 18-487.
Tunstall, James, Quebec, April 30, 1788.—Money Book, 59-246.
Turing, Inglis, Jamaica, September 11, 1772.—Money Book, 52-40.
Turner, Mr., Barbadoes, October 27, 1795.—Money Book, 61-42.
Turquan, Paul, South Carolina, May 1, 1766.—Money Book, 50-2.
Tustian, Peter, clerk, Carolina, November 4, 1719.—Money Book, 27-153.
Tutty, William, Nova Scotia, May 2, 1749.—Money Book, 43-73.
Twyning, William, Caharra (?), in Bahamas, May 1, 1787.—Money Book, 58-53.
Tyler, John, Connecticut, June 30, 1768.—Money Book, 51-79.
Tyrell, John, Jamaica, January 4, 1770.—Money Book, 51-249.

Emigrant Ministers to America 61

Underwood, Thomas Montserrat, November 15, 1791.—Money Book, 60-91.
Urmstons, John, Virginia, June 29, 1722.—Money Book, 29-203.
Urquhart, John, Maryland, February 6, 1732-1733.—Money Book, 36-480.
Urquhart, William, clerk, New York, January 29, 1703-1704.—Money Book, 17-70.
Usher, Arthur, Plantations, February 10, 1736-1737.—Money Book, 38-33.
Usher, John, South Carolina, February 14, 1722-1723.—Money Book, 30-78. Grandson of Hekekiah Usher; son of John Usher. Died April 30, 1775, aged eighty-six (Sprague).

Vardill, John, New York, April 26, 1774.—Money Book, 52-41. M.A. 1774. Died Rector of Skirbeck, Lincolnshire, 1811, aged fifty-nine (Foster).
Vasey, William, clerk, New York, January 22, 1714-1715.—Money Book, 23-438.
Vaugh, Abner, Virginia, March 14, 1771.—Money Book, 52-40.
Vaughan, Edward, Jerseys, April 12, 1709.—Money Book, 19-471.
Venn, John, Jamaica, July 25, 1744.—Money Book, 41-4.
Vere, William, Virginia, October 5, 1771.—Money Book, 52-40.
Vernod, Francis, South Carolina, August 7, 1723.—Money Book, 30-78.
Viets, —, New England, April 22, 1763.—Money Book, 48-272.
Villette, John, Georgia, September 25, 1771.—Money Book, 52-40.

Wagoner, Peter, Maryland, January 14, 1702-1703.—Money Book, 16-251.
Walbanke, —, clerk, Jamaica, April 25, 1699.—Money Book, 14-351.
Walcott, John, Jamaica, July 6, 1769.—Money Book, 51-249.
Walker, —, clerk, Virginia, August 31, 1699.—Money Book, 14-420.
Walker, Robert, Barbadoes, March 10, 1714-1715.—Money Book, 23-496.
Walker, Robert, Maryland, schoolmaster, April 8, 1707.—Money Book, 18-446.
Walker, Thomas, South Carolina, February 28, 1772.—Money Book, 52-40.
Walker, Philip, Maryland, April 8, 1756—Money Book, 45-111.
Waller, William, New England, March 10, 1764.—Money Book, 49-182.

Wallis, Samuel, clerk, Virginia, September 8, 1709.—Money Book, 20-130.
Walls, Benjamin, Maryland, January 11, 1697-1698.—Money Book, 13-424.
Walton, William, Bermudas, April 21, 1741.—Money Book, 40-20.
Ward, Samuel, South Carolina, December 17, 1767.—Money Book, 50-234.
Warner, Samuel, Maryland, schoolmaster, June 12, 1716.—Money Book, 24-409.
Warner, Joseph, St. Christopher's, June 6, 1788.—Money Book, 59-246.
Warren, Thomas, Musquito Shore, June 30, 1768.—Money Book, 51-79.
Warren, Samuel Fenner, South Carolina, January 18, 1758.—Money Book, 46-62.
Warrington, Thomas, Virginia, October 14, 1747.—Money Book, 42-52.
Wasston, Josiah, Antigua, January 18, 1775.—Money Book, 53-172.
Watkins, Hezekiah, New York, October 11, 1744.—Money Book, 41-420.
Watson, Leonard, Virginia, March 24, 1762.—Money Book, 48-155.
Watts, Richard, Virginia, May 10, 1727.—Money Book, 33-307.
Webb, William, Virginia, April 7, 1747.—Money Book, 42-52.
Weeks, Richard, clerk, Jamaica, May 21, 1707.—Money Book, 18-465.
West, John, Jamaica, November 24, 1785.—Money Book, 58-53.
West, William, Virginia, November 28, 1761.—Money Book, 48-155. Born about 1739, Fairfax County, Valencia; died March 30, 1791 (Sprague).
Weston, Martin, Tortola, June 8, 1798.—Money Book, 61-42.
Wetmore, James, America, August 5, 1723.—Money Book, 30-78.
Weyman, Robert, Pennsylvania, October 1, 1719.—Money Book, 27-268.
Wharton, Gilbert, clerk, Berbadoes, July 8, 1701.—Money Book, 15-458.
Wharton, Thomas, Berbadoes, June 24, 1760.—Money Book, 47-108.
Wharton, William, Berbadoes, March 4, 1728-1729 —Money Book, 34-340.

Emigrant Ministers to America 63

Wheatley, Henry, clerk, South Carolina, March 6, 1716-1717.
—Money Book, 25-224.
Wheeler, Wolland, Massachusetts, January 7, 1766 or 1768.—
Money Book, 50-234.
Whinston, —, clerk, North Carolina, September 1, 1709.—
Money Book, 20-126.
Whitaker, Nathaniel, Maryland, February 4, 1741-1742.—
Money Book, 40-20.
White, Alexander, Virginia, June 12, 1745.—Money Book,
41-420.
White, William, Jamaica, October 14, 1728.—Money Book,
34-189.
White, Mr., Pennsylvania, May 19, 1772.—Money Book, 52-40.
Son of Colonel William White. Born in Philadelphia,
March 26, 1748; died July 17, 1836.
Whitehead, John, clerk, Charlestown, South Carolina, catechist and assistant, April 30, 1714.— Money Book,
23-90.
Wicket, Richard, Barbadoes, October 23, 1803.—Money Book,
63-15.
Wilkinson, Thomas, Virginia, August 8, 1753.—Money Book,
44-33.
Wilkinson, Stephen, Maryland, January 24, 1725-1726.—
Money Book, 32-145.
Williams, Raby, Jamaica, January 20, 1806.—Money Book,
63-15. Son of John Meyrick Williams, of Jamaica.
Matriculated 1788 (Foster).
Williams, Charles, Maryland, August 27, 1703.—Money Book,
16-432.
Williamson, Alexander, Maryland, October 10, 1710.—Money
Book, 20-397.
Williamson, Alexander, Maryland, April 8, 1756.—Money
Book, 45-111.
Williamson, Christopher, clerk, Maryland, February 24, 1710-1711.—Money Book, 21-24.
Williamson, James, clerk, Maryland, January 21, 1712-1713.—
Money Book, 22-137.
Willoughby, Edward Chapman, Nova Scotia, February 22,
1793.—Money Book, 60-91.
Wills, John, North Carolina, February 9, 1769.—Money Book,
51-79.
Wilmer, James, Maryland, September 25, 1773.—Money Book,
52-41. James Jones, son of Michael Wilmer, of Kent,
Maryland. Matriculated 1768 (Foster).
Wilson, Francis, Virginia, February 4, 1773.—Money Book,
52-41.

Wilson, Hugh, Pennsylvania, January 2, 1766.—Money Book, 50-2.

Wilson, Thomas, M.A., Antigua, January 27, 1729-1730.—Treasury Board Papers, vol. 273-12. Son of John Wilson, of Evesham, Worcester. M.A. 1723 (Foster).

Wilton, Joseph Dacre Appleby, South Carolina, October 28, 1761.—Money Book, 48-155. Son of Anthony Wilton, of Kirk Levington, Cumberland, clerk. Matriculated 1761 (Foster).

Winder, Thomas, Island of Nevis, September 24, 1724.—Money Book, 31-51.

Wingate, John, Virginia, October 5, 1771.—Money Book, 52-40.

Wingate, Joseph, New England, April 22, 1763.—Money Book, 48-272.

Winslow, Edward, New England, April 23, 1755.—Money Book, 45-111.

Winteley, John, South Carolina, August 3, 1726.—Money Book, 32-145.

Wishart, John, Virginia, July 11, 1764.—Money Book, 49-306.

Wiswall, John, Massachusetts Bay, February 25, 1765.—Money Book, 49-306.

Wogan, John Christopher, —— in Nova Scotia, June 27, 1786. Money Book, 58-53.

Wood, Henry, Newfoundland, July 23, 1802.—Money Book, 63-15. Son of John Wood, of Milton Abbas, Dorset, clerk. B.A. 1791.

Wood, Alexander, clerk, Carolina, June 6, 1707.—Money Book, 18-487.

Wood, William, New Jersey, October 5, 1749.—Money Book, 43-73.

Woodham, Robert Short, Jamaica, January 5, 1787.—Money Book, 58-53.

Woodmason, Charles, South Carolina, May 1, 1766.—Money Book, 50-2.

Woodside, Frederick, Virginia, April 21, 1708.—Money Book, 19-244.

Wooton, James, Maryland, August 12, 1703.—Money Book, 16-422.

Worden, Samuel, clerk, Virginia, March 27, 1712.—Money Book, 21-470.

Wosston, Josiah, Antigua, January 18, 1775.—Money Book, 53-172.

Wright, John, Maryland, March 25, 1729.—Treasury Board Papers, vol. 270-46. Warrant dated June 4, 1729.—Money Book, 34-428.

Wright, George, clerk, Leeward Islands, October 26, 1705.—Money Book, 18-56.
Wye, William, Carolina, August 9, 1717.—Money Book, 25-328.

Yancey, Robert, Virginia, July 28, 1768.—Money Book, 51-79.
Yates, Robert, Virginia, July 6, 1741.—Order Book, 17-318.
Yates, —, clerk, Virginia, January 3, 1698-1699.—Money Book, 14-277.
Yates, —, clerk, Virginia, September 18, 1700.—Money Book, 15-175.
Yates, William, Virginia, April 23, 1742.—Money Book, 41-4.
Yates, Bartholomew, Virginia, June 13, 1737.—Money Book, 39-17. Son of Bartholomew Yates, of Virginia. B.A. 1735 (Foster).
Yong, James, Leeward Islands, December 10, 1695.—Money Book, 13-43.
Young, George, Montserrat, January 26, 1776.—Money Book, 53-172.

Zouberbuhler, Bartholomew, Georgia, February 4, 1745-1746.—Money Book, 42-52.

THE END

www.ingramcontent.com/pod-product-compliance
Lightning Source LLC
Chambersburg PA
CBHW020254090426
42735CB00010B/1918